SETH
BULLOCK

Laura Ingalls Wilder

by Pamela Smith Hill

Wild Bill Hickok and Calamity Jane

by James D. McLaird

Seth Bullock

by David A. Wolff

SETH BULLOCK

BLACK HILLS LAWMAN

DAVID A. WOLFF

South Dakota
State Historical
Society Press
Pierre

Seth Bullock is Volume 3 in the South Dakota Biography Series.

 This publication is funded, in part, by the Deadwood
Publications Fund provided by the City of Deadwood and
the Deadwood Historic Preservation Commission.

Library of Congress Cataloging-in-Publication Data
Wolff, David A.
Seth Bullock : Black Hills lawman / by David A. Wolff.
    p. cm. — (South Dakota biography series ; 3)
Includes bibliographical references and index.
ISBN 978-0-9798940-5-3
1. Bullock, Seth, 1849-1919. 2. Marshals—South Dakota—
Biography. 3. Frontier and pioneer life—South Dakota. I. Title.
HV7911.B8W65 2009
363.28'2092—dc22
[B]
        2008054154

Printed in the United States of America
The paper in this book meets the guidelines for permanence
and durability of the committee on Production Guidelines for
Book Longevity of the Council on Library Resources.

Text and cover design by Rich Hendel

Please visit our website at http://www.sdshspress.com

19 18   5

For those who led me into

Black Hills history:

WATSON PARKER, BOB LEE,

and JOE DOUDA

Contents

Acknowledgements

A project like this incurs many debts, and I need to thank many people. First is Nancy Tystad Koupal at the South Dakota State Historical Society Press. She envisioned the South Dakota Biography Series, which was the motivation for this book. A number of people helped by doing research, sending copies, and answering questions. Ken Stewart, Marvene Riis, and Carol Jennings at the State Archives at the South Dakota State Historical Society in Pierre provided timely information. My friends at Black Hills State University assisted me in countless ways. Librarian Karen Stacy was extremely helpful in getting interlibrary loan material, explaining the horse business, and providing microfilm. Bobbi Sago in the university's Case Library for Western Historical Studies made the book stacks and the Lawrence County tax records available, and Amber Wilde helped with book problems. I also appreciated the support of Kathleen Parrow, Dean Myers, and the Faculty Research Committee, who provided research time. Two students also helped greatly. Stephanie Dickson checked microfilm, and Jim Holmes diligently reviewed the Butte County property records. At the Adams Museum and House, Arlette Hansen gathered information, and Mary Kopco made the Remer diaries available.

A number of experts at archives and museums helped in smaller but important ways. These include Linda Velder at the Newell Museum, Harry Thompson and Gary Olson at the Center for Western Studies at Augustana College, Leslie Waggener at the University of Wyoming's American Heritage Center, David Turk at the United States Marshals Office, Mike Runge and Kevin Kuchenbecker at the Deadwood Historic Preservation Office, and the staff at the North Dakota State Archives and Library.

The people I need to thank the most are my friends. Rich Clow referred me to collections; Ivan Hovland and I spent a day searching property records; Dale Martin answered endless questions about Montana history; and Jerry Bryant went above and beyond the call of duty. He supplied newspaper articles, census data, and unending wisecracks. Kathy Wolff read parts of the manuscript and provided moral support, and my daughter Sarah brought me some important material from the Library of Congress. My younger daughter Shana provided less tangible but still significant support.

I thank them all for helping, and I apologize to those whom I forgot to mention. Their assistance made this book possible, but, of course, all mistakes are my own.

Introduction

Black Hills visitors often associate three names with Deadwood's Wild West past: Wild Bill Hickok, Calamity Jane, and Seth Bullock. Bill's and Jane's connections with Deadwood were fleeting and based on happenstance. They died nearby and were buried in Deadwood's Mount Moriah Cemetery. Luck, however, had nothing to do with Seth Bullock's notoriety. He worked hard for his community. He served as sheriff, started a hardware store, developed a ranch, acted as a town promoter, ran a mining company, volunteered for the Spanish-American War, supervised a national forest, and befriended a president. By the time he died in 1919, these activities had made him famous, at least locally, but tourists and residents today mostly associate him with the Bullock Hotel or the "Seth Bullock" character in the HBO *Deadwood* series. Bullock, however, was more than that. He deserves to be recognized as one of Deadwood's most famous citizens—and not just because he died there.

As this book will show, a few other people, such as Harris Franklin, James K. P. Miller, and Sol Star, probably contributed more to Deadwood's long-term viability than Bullock did. But Bullock did more for the Black Hills in general than any other person. For instance, he founded Belle Fourche and successfully managed the Black Hills Forest Reserve and the United States marshal's office in South Dakota. Without a doubt, he was the most important person in the Black Hills during his lifetime.

What motivated this ambitious man? Greed played a part. He wanted to get ahead, but Bullock also saw himself as an agent of progress, someone whose mission was to help the region and country advance. He made this notion clear when he talked about membership in the Society of Black Hills

Pioneers. This group, he wrote, should honor people who had blazed a trail "for the march of the Nation's progress."[1]

The eight chapters of this book are organized into three parts, each of which covers an era in Bullock's life. In his early years, Bullock saw western advancement as dependent upon order. While operating a store, he wanted to bring law and order to the frontier, and the governor of Dakota Territory obligingly appointed him as Lawrence County's first sheriff in 1877. Bullock, however, was not a man of the people, and he lost his bid for reelection. Although he continued as a deputy United States marshal, the defeat as sheriff allowed him to enter business more actively during the second period of his life. For the next fifteen years, Bullock invested in multiple ventures, from mines to horses, seeking prosperity for himself and the Black Hills, with mixed results. When fire destroyed some of his holdings, he changed course again and volunteered for the Spanish-American War. This episode in his life gained him national attention and ultimately a federal job as a forest supervisor. He still sought order and progress for the Hills, but he did it through administering regulations. In the final official role in his life, Bullock served as United States marshal under two presidents. From the time he arrived in the Black Hills to the moment of his death, Bullock worked to advance the area, but what that meant and how he did it changed over the years.

Beyond highlighting the major trends in Bullock's life, this narrative tries to accomplish some smaller tasks, such as countering myths. For example, Bullock did not marry his brother's wife, he did not found Yellowstone National Park, and he did not die in the Bullock Hotel. This book also illuminates the risks that came with frontier investments. Just as Deadwood went from boom to bust, Bullock himself enjoyed times of prosperity and periods of failure. While this text does not try to psychoanalyze the man, it does touch upon his personal idiosyncrasies. Bullock had a good sense of humor. Unfortunately, few of his "jokes" made it into print, and only a small sampling appear here. Bullock liked to drink, and some Deadwood observers criticized him for that tendency. Limited accounts of his drinking, however, actually exist. And finally, many people knew him, but only a handful called him a friend. In fact, he had several enemies, and references to those are included here, as well.[2]

Writing a book about Seth Bullock would seem a simple task. After all, his grandson, Kenneth Kellar, used Bullock's papers to publish *Seth Bullock, Frontier Marshal*; Bullock himself wrote a brief narrative about his early years in Lawrence County; and many Black Hills history volumes mention him. Unfortunately, these sources only scratch the surface of Bullock's life, and worse yet, many of them repeat errors or fabrications. Secondary sources have to be used with care, and I found myself relying on newspapers to fill in the timeline and the major events of Bullock's life. Fortunately, for each era of his life, a variety of secondary sources helped "triangulate" the information. For instance, for the period of the Spanish-American War, two books covered the exploits of Bullock's unit, Grigsby's Cowboys.

Bullock's experiences with Theodore Roosevelt can also be pieced together from a variety of sources, including a book by Kermit Roosevelt. Yet, all documents need to be read carefully. Theodore Roosevelt's autobiographical musings add confusion that only a careful reading of the Roosevelt letters can clarify.[3] Other primary documents, in particular Bullock's own letters, exist in private hands. Unfortunately, I was not allowed access to this material. However, I believe that Bullock's grandson used most of this collection in *Seth Bullock, Frontier Marshal*, making the most important documents available in this form. Finally, this volume is not meant to be the definitive biography of Bullock. It is too brief, but I hope it gives readers a good appreciation of this important man and of the Black Hills during his lifetime.

While Bullock certainly believed in progress, he also saw himself in the more pragmatic terms of this book's subtitle: as a lawman. In fact, his drive to uphold the law carried on throughout his life. He began his public-service career as a sheriff in Montana Territory and ended it as a United States marshal in South Dakota. His military duty during the Spanish-American War and his time as forest supervisor were extensions of that vocation. Yet, he first came to Deadwood to open a hardware store, and entrepreneurship filled much of his life, although financial success often eluded him. Nevertheless, in 1919 as he honored his recently passed friend Theodore Roosevelt, Bullock could reflect on his own accomplishments with satisfaction. From the town of Belle Fourche to the Bullock Hotel in Deadwood, he had also left a legacy as a builder. He had brought to the Black Hills the progress that he so earnestly desired.

PIONEER
AND
POLITICIAN
1847–1879

1

From Montana
to Deadwood

On 4 July 1876, twenty-nine-year-old Seth Bullock could reflect on his accomplishments with pride. Since his arrival in Montana nine years before, he had served in the territorial legislature, been elected sheriff of Lewis and Clark County, and run a successful business. On this day, he led the officers of the Helena Fire Department in a parade celebrating the nation's centennial. His position and his role as assistant parade marshal reflected his status in the community, and as he strode down the street, all in town recognized him. He stood taller than most others, at six foot one inch, and his lean body had an angular look, accented by a prominent nose and jaw, with a full mustache drooping over his upper lip. Yet, this obviously proud man must have felt some anxiety and anticipation, for in three days, he would leave Montana for the new gold fields in the Black Hills of Dakota Territory.[1]

Whatever doubts he may have held did not come from a fear of failure. Bullock had immense confidence in himself, and he knew that if his Black Hills ventures did not work out, he could always return to Montana. In fact, he reported to a Helena newspaper that he would probably be gone only a matter of weeks, and he told friends that he would remain only as long as he was satisfied. His concern lay more in the uncertainty of the trip and with the situation he might encounter within the Black Hills. Just eight days before the nation's centennial, Lakota and Cheyenne warriors had wiped out Lieutenant Colonel George Armstrong Custer's command at the Little Big Horn, spreading fear across the region that more Indian attacks would follow. Bullock's trip would take him through Lakota country and to its heart, the Black Hills. While Bullock paraded in Helena, the Fourth of July celebrations in the Black Hills mining camps included orations imploring Congress to recognize the miners' claims and remove Indian title to the land. The illegal nature of the gold seekers' invasion of the Black Hills and the hostility of the Indians made any venture into the region risky, and Bullock recognized the dangers.[2]

The hazards of traveling through Indian country were reduced with numbers, and Bullock hoped for company. By the summer of 1876, the trails to the Black Hills always seemed to have travelers on them. Among the earliest venturers to the Black Hills were two hundred men who were known collectively as the "Montana Party." They left Montana three months before Bullock. Some homesteaded along Spearfish Creek on the northern edge of the Black Hills, hoping to profit more from farming than mining. Others built a stockade for horses in Centennial Prairie, a few miles east of Spearfish Creek. Here they tended miners' horses for a fee, and their animals became known as the "Montana Herd." Still others went on to the placer ground within the northern Black Hills along Whitewood and Deadwood creeks, in what was called Deadwood Gulch. Prospectors had discovered gold along these streams in late 1875, and by the spring of 1876, this area had proven to be the richest in the Hills and, consequently, the focus of the rush. Here the Montana men staked placer claims or went into business. James K. P. Miller, for example, came to Deadwood Gulch from Virginia City to open a grocery store and a bank. These men became such a presence in the region that a camp called Montana City developed on Whitewood Creek.[3]

Bullock undoubtedly knew some of these Montana men, and he had heard of their experiences, but the Battle of the Little Big Horn had changed the dynamics along the trails.

The fear of Indian attacks caused many to delay their travels, and new arrivals to Deadwood dropped off dramatically in July and August. But Bullock could not delay because his plans had already been set. While in Montana, he had formed a partnership with thirty-six-year-old Solomon ("Sol") Star. They decided to pool their resources and open a business in Deadwood Gulch. To this end, Star agreed to go east for merchandise, and Bullock, accompanied by another group of men from Montana, promised to meet Star and his purchases as they returned up the Missouri River to Bismarck in northern Dakota Territory. From there, they would transport the wares over the Bismarck Trail to the Black Hills.[4]

The Bismarck Trail had been laid out in December of 1875, and by the summer of 1876, travelers had made it one of the main routes to the Black Hills. Its popularity developed, in part, because Bismarck had two outside connections: Missouri River steamboats and the Northern Pacific Railroad. As the gold rush centered on the northern Black Hills, this trail competed for traffic with the longer routes from Cheyenne, Wyoming, and Sidney, Nebraska. While Indian hostilities after Custer's death made this eastern route more dangerous, Bullock and Star's party made it from Bismarck to the Black Hills without a problem. Their unhampered voyage may have been the result of luck, for as they neared the Hills they came across remnants of a recent Indian attack. Or it may have been unhindered because of the animals they chose. They used oxen to pull their wagons, and the Indians, who did not see as much value in oxen as in horses, may have decided to spend their energy pursuing more promising targets. The number of wagons Bullock and Star required for their trip went unrecorded, but fellow merchant James K. P. Miller had used twenty-three wagons to bring his merchandise to the Black Hills from Bismarck.[5]

It took Bullock's group nearly four weeks to reach the Black Hills from Helena, and on 3 August, the men slowly eased their wagons down the steep hillside into Deadwood Gulch, a perilous drop of several hundred yards.[6] They most likely came down near Elizabethtown, the first camp established along Whitewood Creek. Once at the bottom, Bullock and Star could see the mayhem that the gold rush had produced. A single narrow road wound around tents, cabins, and piles of rock from the nearby placer claims. Whitewood Creek sat just a few yards from their path, but it had no discernible channel as miners continually rerouted it, looking for the gold hidden beneath. And the makeshift road itself looked like a small stream, with runoff water and human waste pooling along its course. Just barely visible in the distance sat Montana City. Above Elizabethtown and virtually connected to it was the embryonic gold camp of Deadwood. Two disgruntled miners, who reportedly did not like the rules in Elizabethtown, had moved up the creek and laid out Deadwood in April 1876. These camps contained about three thousand people when Bullock and Star arrived, and a few miles farther up Whitewood and Deadwood creeks sat other gold camps, such as Gayville and Central City, with the northern Black Hills containing perhaps five thousand people.[7]

Even beyond the typical tumult of a boom camp, Deadwood was a community in an uproar. The day before Bullock and Star arrived, Jack McCall had put a bullet in the back of James Butler ("Wild Bill") Hickok's head, and while violence was common in unregulated mining camps, the death of the noted gunfighter caught the attention of all. Bullock and Star got there just in time to see McCall go free as the jurors of the miners' court found him not guilty. The jury, composed in part of McCall cronies, accepted the murderer's plea of justifiable homicide when he claimed that Hickok had killed his brother. Adding to this turmoil was a heightened fear of Indians. On the day of Hickok's death, a rider entered Deadwood with the head of an Indian recently severed from its body. The rider wanted the bounty some locals had placed on Indians, but the grotesque display caused increased concern about Indians surrounding the northern Hills. None of this mayhem surprised Bullock and Star, for they had seen much of it before in the Montana gold fields.[8]

Bullock and Star had arrived in Montana near the beginning of that region's gold rush, as well, and during their time there, they had witnessed the birth and death of mining camps and the evolution of the gold business, gaining experience that would serve them well in Deadwood. Star beat Bullock to Montana by two years, arriving in 1865. Born in Bavaria in 1840, Star entered the United States at the age of ten and lived in Ohio, Indiana, and Missouri before arriving in the new camp of Helena. Gold had been discovered in Last Chance Gulch just before Star arrived, and Helena soon grew up around it. Looking for better opportunities, Star moved to Virginia City to run a store and then, by 1870, on to Deer Lodge to work as a banker.[9]

Bullock's voyage to Helena began in Ontario, Canada, where he was born in 1847. According to a family history, his father, George, was "an irascible, retired Major in the British Army," who was "a somewhat testy, hard-nosed disciplinarian." On the other hand, his mother, Agnes, was described as a "sweet natured, docile Scotch woman."[10] Either bored or dissatisfied as a child, Seth ran away from home to join a sister who was married to a United States Army officer. He soon returned to his parents but only to flee again. When the Civil War began, he made several attempts to enlist in the Union Army, but he was rejected because of age. Yet, these adventures turned Bullock into a confident adult, who did not back down from a challenge. He was willing to take a chance and intended to succeed at whatever he tried. In other words, he developed a strong personality with firm opinions to match. He befriended people he saw as equals and ignored those he looked down upon. Despite his youthful wanderlust, Bullock acquired a solid education and an appreciation for fine literature. He also gained a thirst for strong drink, which fortunately came with a dry sense of humor.[11] Deadwood resident Estelline Bennett later observed that Bullock had "a soft voice that spoke English like the educated gentleman he was."[12]

During Seth's childhood, his parents moved their family of four boys and three girls from Canada to Michigan, and while he apparently returned periodically to Canada, the time Bullock spent growing up in Michigan proved critical to his future. It allowed him to claim United States citizenship, which became important when he ran for political office, and he met Martha Eccles, who would become his wife. They were childhood sweethearts, and when he left for Montana in 1867, she was fifteen and he was twenty, but their relationship had substance. Seven years after he arrived in Montana, Bullock sent for Martha. She took the train to Utah, the closest rail connection to Montana, and the two were married in Salt Lake City in 1874.[13]

Prior to Martha's arrival, Bullock concentrated on his career, and his efforts in Montana led directly to his activities in Deadwood. When he first arrived in Helena, Bullock formed a partnership with a retail and wholesale grocer named James Gostling. Bullock, however, did not become a full-fledged merchant. He did not appear to like the confining environment of a store. Instead, he primarily worked as an auctioneer and commission merchant. In these activities, he sold merchandise and property for others, without having to invest in inventory himself. These activities also gave Bullock much flexibility; sometimes he worked within the store, but often he traveled, as the job demanded. Eventually he ended his partnership and worked independently as an auctioneer.[14]

Flexibility in business suited Bullock because he had a passion for politics, community leadership, and law enforcement. Bullock always tried to be at the forefront of community issues and projects, such as fire prevention and economic development. He did not take on these activities just for the good of the community, however. He also hoped to benefit. Bullock operated on the principle that general prosperity would bring him success. As well, he realized that progress could not come without proper governance and order.

But when Bullock moved to Montana in 1867, territorial politics were in turmoil. Democrats held the political majority, but Republican presidents sent fellow Republicans to administer the territory. This combination led to ineffective and corrupt administrations, and Bullock immediately worked to improve the situation. Because of his Michigan background, the young man arrived in Montana as a strident Republican, and his assertive stance soon caught the eye of local Republican operatives, such as Cornelius Hedges and William Clagett. After some prodding, they convinced Bullock to seek his party's nomination as a candidate for the territorial legislature in 1867. Since he had just recently arrived and was only twenty years old, Bullock had little chance. The delegates at the Republican convention did not select him to run, but this first setback did not dampen his political ambitions.[15]

In 1871, Bullock tried again, and this time his party's convention nominated him for the territorial council, the upper house of the legislature. Also by this time, Montana politics had settled down. President Ulysses S. Grant had appointed a capable governor in Benjamin Potts, and during his long tenure, Potts brought conciliation between Democrats and Republicans. This calm allowed for Clagett's election as territorial delegate to Congress and for Hedges to become superintendent of public instruction. Bullock similarly prevailed in the August 1871 election, holding his council position until 1873. During this time, he worked to get a railroad built into Montana from Utah, strove to have the capital moved from Virginia City to Helena, and promoted a resolution asking the United States Congress to establish Yellowstone as a national park.[16]

Bullock's efforts on behalf of Yellowstone have become a greatly exaggerated part of his legend. Some authors have used Bullock's actions for Yellowstone Park as an example of his leadership ability and of his desire for natural resource conservation, which became more pronounced later in the Black Hills. They have argued that Bullock's legislation "persuaded" the House of Representatives to approve the Yellowstone measure, giving him much of the credit while ignoring the complex negotiations that actually prevailed.[17] In reality, Bullock had never visited Yellowstone and knew little about it when the debate over park status began in Congress. What he knew came from his Republican associates, Hedges and Clagett. Hedges had toured the park with the Henry D. Washburn Expedition in 1870 and had published articles in the *Helena Herald* extolling the beauty of the area and suggesting its removal from Wyoming to Montana. Clagett, serving as Montana's delegate to Congress, then introduced the Yellowstone Park bill into the House of Representatives in 1871.[18]

As the Yellowstone debate went on, the Montana Legislative Council adopted, on a motion from Bullock, a memorial that asked Congress to add the Yellowstone area to Montana and make it "a great national park."[19] It is unknown whether Bullock wrote the Montana resolution (he may have done so in association with Hedges), and it is not known what actual influence it had on Congress. Yellowstone was not added to Montana, and it was Clagett, Hedges, explorer Ferdinand V. Hayden, Northern Pacific Railroad publicists, and others who persuaded Congress to establish Yellowstone National Park. What is known is that Representative Henry Dawes used the Montana memorial during a committee debate when he explained how the park measure did not interfere with settlers' rights and that the Montana legislature in fact supported it.[20]

Nearly six months after President Grant signed the Yellowstone bill into law, Bullock and three companions took a month-long horseback tour of the new park. He went to verify what he had heard, personally assessing the real value of the area. When it came to conservation, Bullock had a pragmatic side. He advocated that resources be used wisely, with agriculture as a top priority. During the trip, he kept a daily journal for the only time in his life, recording his impressions of the land and its potential. As his small troop arrived at the Yellowstone River north of the park, he wrote: "This portion of the valley not adaptable for farming. Rocky." As he entered the park at Mammoth Hot Springs, he reported that the waters could help treat "blood and rheumatic diseases." A little farther on, however, his eye went from the practical to the esthetic. At Yellowstone Lake, he "stood spellbound by the enchanting scene," while he expressed himself incapable of describing the Grand Canyon and lower falls. He recognized that scenery could have value when he added, "Would like to own 100 acres here a hundred years from now."[21] In the end, Bullock was satisfied with the park, and perhaps inspired by his Yellowstone experience, he would eventually work for the most beneficial use of natural resources.

While Bullock served in the territorial legislature, he also became involved in other aspects of public service. He joined the engine company of the Helena fire department, eventually becoming chief engineer, and he became a deputy sheriff. Then, in 1873, he ran for sheriff of Lewis and Clark County, of which Helena was the county seat, and he secured a sixty-six vote majority out of the nearly one thousand cast in the August election. By the time he became sheriff, the rowdy, frontier stage of the gold rush had mostly passed, and Bullock's tasks reflected a more settled community. When a man, "uttering vague threats," carried a loaded rifle down Main Street, Bullock placed him in jail.[22] As miners gave up and deserted their holdings, Bullock ran sheriff's sales to satisfy claims against their debts. And he presided over the first legal hanging in Montana Territory.[23]

Another legend, perhaps promoted by Bullock himself, surrounds the events of this hanging. As related by Kermit Roosevelt in 1920, an unruly mob, in the tradition of Montana vigilantes, drove off the hangman so they could perform the task themselves. At this point, according to the Roosevelt account, Bullock intervened. While holding the crowd off with a six-shooter, he hanged the man himself. The 1875 Helena newspapers, however, told a slightly different story. Contrary to territorial law, which specified that hangings must be done out of public view with only invited guests to serve as witnesses, as many as a thousand people climbed onto the roofs of surrounding buildings to view the event, but the hanging apparently went off without a problem. Sheriff Bullock had deputized a number of the official witnesses in case of trouble.[24] Two months later, Bullock presided over a second hanging, and a Helena newspaper stressed that it transpired with few observers and "deep solemnity."[25] Indeed, later in life, Bullock enjoyed talking about these hangings, and he may have told Roosevelt the embellished account to impress him with tales of the frontier and his own heroics. On another occasion, however, as he detailed the events to an enthralled listener, Bullock admitted that killing the two men affected him to the point where he nearly gave up politics.[26]

Shortly after the second hanging, Bullock's term as sheriff ended, and he did not run for reelection. The reason is unknown. Perhaps the hangings did make him think twice about the job. Or, it could have been that Republican operatives wanted to give another party member the chance to serve. Whatever the reason, Bullock remained active in the Republican party, and his zealousness caught the attention of the local press. The *Helena Daily Independent* labeled Bullock and his Republican associates "brethren in the faith," with Bullock gaining the title of "Bishop."[27] Bullock accepted the nickname and used it until he left for the Black Hills, where the title disappeared. Bullock appears to have consciously dropped the nickname, perhaps indicating the hope for a fresh start.

When Bullock entered politics in 1871, he met Sol Star. Although he did not have an official position, Star had attended the legislative session in Virginia City in December. Housing was in short supply, and by happenstance, Bullock, Star, and two other men rented a room together. Because of the room's small size, the roommates ordered a bedstead that held all four. After five weeks of sharing political insights, living space, and a warm bed, Bullock and Star established a friendship. In 1872, President Grant appointed Star register of the United States Land Office in Helena, and in 1874, Star became territorial auditor. This job lasted until 1875 when Star returned to the mercantile and banking business in Helena. Similarly, as Bullock's term as sheriff ended in 1875, he reestablished himself there as an auctioneer. As Republicans, politicians, and businessmen, Bullock and Star got to know each other well, and as word of gold in the Black Hills spread, they decided to form a partnership and head for the new country.[28]

After investing nearly ten years apiece in Montana, Bullock and Star did not leave lightly, but they, like many people in the nation, felt the effects of the Panic of 1873. The economic hardships that began with the panic caused banks to fail and agricultural prices to drop. In Montana, the downturn seemed all the more troublesome as no new gold discoveries had been made and mining declined.[29] Bullock and Star experienced this economic distress as they reentered the business world in 1875. Better times, however, did not seem far away. In the summer of 1874, Lieutenant Colonel Custer had led a large expedition through the Black Hills, and prospectors with the troops reported gold discoveries. This news stimulated a rush, with a few gold seekers entering the Hills illegally in late 1874 and many more following throughout 1875.

Bullock and Star did not rush to the Black Hills with the first wave of prospectors, and they probably hesitated for a couple of reasons. First, they wanted to see how the gold field panned out. Throughout the West, many gold discoveries, which stimulated rushes, turned out to be false or overstated, financially ruining those who hurried in. Second, Bullock and Star recognized that the government was making an effort to enforce the Fort Laramie Treaty of 1868, which stipulated that whites could not enter the Great Sioux Reservation, including the Black Hills. To this end, Brigadier General George Crook led a troop of soldiers through the Black Hills to remove the trespassing prospectors in the summer of 1875. By the next summer, reports confirmed that real value existed in the northern Black Hills, and the government had withdrawn the military patrols, having found it impossible to control the prospectors, effectively opening the region to settlement.[30]

Also by the summer of 1876, Bullock and Star had figured out the nature of their partnership. They agreed to open a hardware store, run an auction house, and build a fireproof storage facility. This latter activity came from their mining-camp experience. All boomtowns had a tendency to burn; Helena burned six times from 1869 to 1874; and many who came to a gold camp would pay to have their supplies securely stashed away. Star would take the lead in running the store. He fit the part of the quiet, "inside man," meaning he could effectively handle the day-to-day business. Bullock, on the other hand, found stores confining, but his expertise as an auctioneer proved a valuable asset. Bullock also had a stronger personality than Star, allowing him to work more as an "outside man," doing what was necessary in the community to make sure their business succeeded. In reality, they probably could have done well individually, but a partnership reduced risk and allowed them to pool resources, with Star bringing more capital into the enterprise. His role as shopkeeper and as majority investor ensured that his name would be listed first in their various undertakings, such as the Star and Bullock Hardware.[31]

Beyond opening a business, Bullock and Star undoubtedly left for the Black Hills with political ambitions. Both men had been involved in politics in Montana, but they found the going tough in that strongly Democratic territory. The Black Hills offered new opportunities. Counties and possibly a new territory would be established, and new government jobs would follow, offering three incentives for people such as Bullock and Star. First, these positions provided steady income in an economically uncertain environment. Second, as positions of leadership, they also provided the law and order necessary for a town to succeed and for merchants, such as themselves, to prosper. And, finally, the two men enjoyed public service. Because of these reasons, both men would remain active in politics throughout their Black Hills careers.

Bullock had one other consideration before he could leave Montana. About a year after Martha and Seth married, they had their first child, Margaret, born in August 1875. With Margaret not yet one year old, Bullock did not want to leave his wife and daughter in Helena, and he did not want to take them to the rough-and-tumble gold camp. Instead, his wife and daughter headed east. They would stay with Martha's parents in Tecumseh, Michigan, until Bullock judged the time right for them to return west. Martha and Margaret's trip east, however, provided some excitement. They caught a Missouri River steamboat 130 miles northeast of Helena at Fort Benton. When they reached the Cheyenne River Agency in Dakota Territory, Lakota warriors, apparently agitated over the Black Hills gold rush, boarded the boat, walked throughout, peered into the cabin windows, but did no harm. This brush with danger impressed Martha enough that all her family heard the story, and it was included in her obituary sixty-three years later. After that incident, the rest of the trip to Michigan was quiet, and Martha waited there for her husband to send for her once again.[32]

With his family safely in Michigan and his business partnership established, Bullock headed to the Black Hills. Once he and Star arrived and stood at the bottom of Deadwood Gulch, new considerations confronted them, such as where was the best place to start a business. After a quick overview, the camp of Deadwood seemed the most promising. It sat at the confluence of Deadwood and Whitewood creeks, seemingly at the center of the action, and next to it another mining camp, known as South Deadwood, was beginning to emerge. Bullock wanted to start business immediately, and as an auctioneer, he knew just what to do. As a family story goes, on the night he and Star arrived, Bullock began auctioning off chamber pots, an item they apparently had in excess. In reality, he probably auctioned off anything he could sell at a profit, for the two men brought everything a mining man could want, including axes, picks, shovels, dynamite, rope, fry pans, and Dutch ovens. No matter what he sold that evening, the two partners were in business.[33]

The next day Bullock and Star purchased a partially completed two-story building on a corner lot on Main Street, where a small and ill-defined side street named Wall Street entered. Sitting parallel to Whitewood Creek, Main Street was Deadwood's primary thoroughfare. Freight wagons, animals, and foot traffic constantly jammed its half-mile course, and at Deadwood's upper end, the road curved into South Deadwood. Some cross streets had been established, such as Wall Street, but aspiring business owners, desperate for locations, often set up shops in these right-of-ways. By the time Bullock and Star arrived, each side of Main Street was crowded with buildings, some of them two- and three-story frame structures, rapidly constructed out of rough, green lumber. These buildings reflected a sense of impermanence, and with many of them built on active placer claims, their destruction in the on-going search for gold seemed guaranteed. Main Street served not only as the primary thoroughfare but also as a cesspool of human and animal waste.[34] Early visitors described it as having a nauseating odor, with the knee-deep mud of such a consistency that it was a "matter of life and death" to cross.[35]

The conditions did not deter Bullock and Star, and their location proved to be a good one. Situated not far below the confluence of creeks, their building sat at the heart of Deadwood's business district. Here, as the Deadwood Pioneer reported, the two men opened "an auction, commission, and storage house,"[36] and Star and Bullock Hardware soon followed. This site would be the home of the partners' business activities for the next two decades, and the intersection of Main and Wall streets became known locally as the Star and Bullock corner.[37] Years later, Bullock referred to it as "old '76 corner."[38]

Success, however, was not guaranteed, and before they could prosper, Bullock and Star needed to come to terms with Deadwood. A little over a month after he arrived, Bullock expressed some frustrations with the camp in a letter he wrote to an associate in Montana. While he called Deadwood a "red hot" mining town, he went on to relate his concern over the poor business environment. Too many men had come to the area for the amount of work available, he claimed, and an abundance of supplies had made "trade dull."[39] A count in September 1876 found eleven clothing stores, twenty-one grocers, and twenty-seven saloons, but only two hardware stores and four auctioneers. The abundance of some businesses caused high prices to drop, but Bullock and Star seemingly occupied a less-crowded niche.[40]

Bullock's greater concern seemed to be with violence. He stated: "We have no law and no order, and no prospect of either. Several murders have been committed and nothing done."[41] Indeed the Black Hills, and especially Deadwood, attracted a large lawless class, people who saw the isolation and the absence of law as an advantage for their trade. Some even came to the Hills to escape prosecution for crimes committed elsewhere. Just as Bullock arrived in Deadwood, two large gambling operations, financed with money from Chicago and Montana, had opened on lower Main Street, bringing more turmoil to the town.[42] One early historian suggested that Deadwood represented a miner's "heaven, or perhaps a hell," as music, gambling, shooting, and fights went on day and night.[43] Bullock and Star accepted some disorder, but they knew that success would come only with social order.

Other commentators suspected that any success in Deadwood would be fleeting. A reporter from Scribner's magazine declared that the lack of rail connections and the harsh climate would bring only failure to the Black Hills. Other visitors declared that Deadwood's location was too inconvenient and too confined by the gulch, especially for railroads, to afford any chance of survival. While the economy may have appeared robust in 1876, doomsayers forecasted that the population would soon move on to other settings, leaving Deadwood a ghost town. While Bullock recognized the possibility of failure, he and Star bet on the town's permanence by buying their building, unlike many other businessmen who chose to rent.[44]

Bullock had no intention of failing. He knew that many

of the problems were within his power to mediate. Plus, he detected some positives in Deadwood. In terms of violence, miners' meetings and miners' courts existed to deal with the murderers. Although the ad-hoc nature of these gatherings limited what they could do (they seldom found anyone guilty), they still prevented vigilantism from breaking out in the Hills during the gold-rush era, unlike in Montana. In fact, Bullock came to realize that violence was somewhat self-limiting in Deadwood where everyone carried weapons, and the fear of retaliation prevented bloodshed.[45]

Bullock also saw positive economic developments in 1876. In late July, prospectors had uncovered a deeper pay streak in the placer mines, from eight to fifteen feet below the surface, encouraging him to say that the new finds might create a "permanent mining district."[46] He also recognized that a number of hardrock claims had been located not far from Deadwood. For instance, the Manuel brothers had staked the Homestake claim just a few miles above town in April 1876, and early reports sounded encouraging. While most hardrock miners initially lacked the equipment to treat the ore, crushing machinery began arriving in the fall of 1876, and Bullock anticipated that these discoveries would bring a new round of development and prosperity. Even without hardrock mining, the people in Deadwood saw the placer diggings produce nearly two million dollars in gold by October 1876. The mineral prospects certainly encouraged Bullock and Star.[47]

As they put down roots in Deadwood, the two partners undoubtedly experienced mixed emotions. They had already lived through boomtown uncertainties in Montana, and in Dakota Territory, they stepped into the unknown again. Except, this time they came fully aware of what needed to be done to make a profit and to turn this boom camp into a city of permanence. Success now required order, and Bullock took the lead to make that happen.

2

Establishing the Law

Just as Bullock and Star did, many others in Deadwood recognized that the periodic miners' meetings and miners' courts could not bring the order that the burgeoning town and its growing population needed. New community problems had developed, and a number of people wanted some type of committee, with sweeping mandates, to take charge. A few saw a fire control committee as essential, not only because of the large number of log and frame structures and the many wood stoves they contained, but also because of the numerous campfires consistently burning up and down the gulch. Others wanted a formal committee that would prevent merchants from squatting in the side streets. The final impetus came when disease threatened the camp. As word spread that a gambler, recently arrived from Cheyenne, Wyoming, had brought smallpox, all wanted action.

After discussing the issue at two meetings, the miners voted on 14 August to establish a five-member committee known as the Board of Health and Street Commissioners. Its tasks included watching for fires, removing obstructions from streets, and building a pest house. In actuality, the committee took control of Deadwood, with the understanding that miners' meetings would still convene to consider larger problems and to support the Board of Health when necessary. For instance, the board was given authority to solicit funds; if any camp inhabitants refused to contribute, they were to be reported at the next miners' meeting. Similarly, if a board's decision met resistance, the miners guaranteed to support the committee, with guns if necessary.[1]

Among the five commissioners selected was Seth Bullock. The choice seems a little surprising, considering that Bullock arrived in Deadwood just eleven days before the committee was organized. Yet, it also says much about the man. First, he had some fame. The large contingent of Montana men in the gulch knew and trusted Bullock, and they undoubtedly supported his selection. Second, he wanted the job. With it, he hoped to bring some order to the camp so that legitimate businesses could thrive. It also constituted his first step into local politics, establishing him as a leader. The five commissioners shared the board's responsibilities, and all were considered fire wardens, but Bullock took on extra jobs, such as becoming treasurer.[2]

Concern over a potential smallpox epidemic rapidly became the board's top priority. Once the commissioners determined that the illness was a contagious disease, they decided to build a pest house to keep the afflicted away from the general population. Bullock and the other commissioners solicited gold dust to buy lumber and then recruited volunteer carpenters. Their biggest problem came with finding a building location. The board first selected a site one-half mile above Elizabethtown, but residents there protested, saying it was nothing more than an effort to kill their young camp, perhaps literally. Besides, that location sat near the water supply of a local brewery, and all could see the wisdom of putting the pest house elsewhere. They next selected a spot a mile from town, near the Spearfish road, but Indian raids negated this site. The board then began construction at a third locale near the town's cemetery, above the newly formed camp of South Deadwood. The people there actively protested this decision by cutting away the wooden foundations of the partially completed structure.

The Board of Health felt little concern for the few residents of South Deadwood and decided to hold this position, with force if necessary. At this point, cooler heads prevailed and a miners' meeting was called to resolve the impasse. The meeting avoided violence with a compromise. The people of South Deadwood volunteered to move the building to Spruce Gulch, below Deadwood, and finish its construction, thereby moving the building away from their neighborhood and compensating for the damage they had done. This solution also relieved the Board of Health from finishing what had become a two-week project and a nuisance unto itself. By the time the pest house opened, only two smallpox cases remained. During the location fight, a vaccine had arrived from Sidney, Nebraska.[3]

While trying to find a location for the pest house, Bullock and the Board of Health responded to other events as they arose. On Sunday, 20 August, word spread through Deadwood that more than one hundred Indians had attacked the Montana Herd on Centennial Prairie, making off with a large number of horses. Deadwood was teeming with prospectors and miners who came to town on Sundays to buy supplies and relax, and they suddenly wanted revenge. Armed riders, many fortified by alcohol, soon rushed out of town to chase the Indians and recover the stolen horses. While Bullock did not join these men, he had to deal with the aftermath of both the raid and the pursuit.

Death haunted that Sunday, and at least four Deadwood-area residents lost their lives. One was Henry Weston ("Preacher") Smith. His body was found on the road to nearby Crook City, where he had planned to deliver a Sunday service. Some historians argue that road agents or robbers killed Smith and not Indians, but the events of that day implicate the latter. Indians certainly killed the other three men, two of whom had entered into the pursuit. As the bodies were returned to Deadwood, the Board of Health, in the absence of any other authority, made plans to bury those who did not have family and friends in town, including Preacher Smith.[4]

Smith's interment gained special notice. He had come to the Hills for the gold rush, but when he saw an absence of religion, his Methodist training compelled him to spend every Sunday standing on a box along Main Street, spreading the word of God. During the week, Smith worked at odd jobs, with most people regarding him as an honest and conscientious man. The board wanted to do right by him in death. They first investigated the site of his murder, where they found little evidence of the guilty party. The commissioners next drew straws to see who would conduct a proper religious ceremony at Smith's grave, and Bullock pulled the short one, much to his dismay. He had never met Preacher Smith, and he was not a religious man. In the nick of time, a deacon from a Congregational church showed up and performed the service. Bullock, however, wrote a letter of condolence to a friend of Smith's in Louisville, Kentucky, and sent Smith's Bible to the preacher's sister in Memphis, Tennessee.[5]

Disasters also befell American Indians because of the 20 August attack on the Montana Herd. A number died, and in one unfortunate incident, a local man known as Texas Jack beheaded a dead Indian, then raced to Deadwood on that same Sunday, yelling and waving the bloody head. To profit from his prize, he began selling locks of hair, an action that revolted the Board of Health. They took possession of the head and paid Jack a bounty.[6] According to Bullock, they justified their action "on the theory that the killing of the Indians was conducive to the health of the community." Bullock and other board members promptly buried the head.[7]

Just as this excitement settled down, more developed. On 22 August, Harry ("Sam") Young, bartender at Saloon No. 10, shot to death Myer Baum, known as "Bummer Dan." Young's intended target, however, had been Sam Hartman, or "Laughing Sam," a man of low repute, who had previously threatened to kill him. Baum, not knowing the intensity of the hatred and hoping to play a joke on his friend Young, wore Laughing Sam's distinctive overcoat into Young's bar. In the poor light inside the saloon, Young thought Sam had arrived to kill him, and he grabbed his gun and shot, killing Baum. Recognizing his mistake, Young immediately turned himself over to the Board of Health for trial, claiming that the shooting was accidental. A trial was beyond the board's power, so a miners' court was convened to try the case. Bullock, acting as sheriff, summoned the jurors for the murder trial. After two days of testimony, the jury deliberated for three and one-half hours, finding Young "not guilty of the crime charged." They based their decision on the fact that Young and Baum had been friends and that Young had no intention of killing him.[8]

After three weeks of handling nearly every crisis in camp, the Board of Health recognized the need for a more formal governing body, and the commissioners called a miners' meeting to consider forming a city government. To many people, it seemed about time. The Black Hills Pioneer of Deadwood desperately wanted a city council and city ordinances, arguing that an effective government would put the town on the "road to prosperity and honor."[9] More practically, Bullock realized that the federal government no longer threatened to remove the trespassing settlers and that the residents could and should take steps for formal organization. He also recognized that an organized government might increase law and order. Others in town just thought it made sense because of the increasing population. But all recognized the provisional nature of any government they formed, for they still occupied the Black Hills illegally.[10]

The miners' meeting agreed to form a city government and set elections for 11 September, asking residents to vote for or against organization and to select city officials, including councilmen and a marshal. The meeting also invited the three connected camps of Deadwood, Elizabethtown, and

South Deadwood to be a part of the new government, but South Deadwood refused, wishing to remain an independent borough for the time being. When the election came, the vote was overwhelming, with 1,082 in favor of a city government and 57 against, indicating a strong preference for more regulation. With this action, the miners' meetings came to an end, and the Board of Health went out of business. Bullock was not part of the new government. He chose not to run, even for the position of marshal. Instead, Sol Star ran for the council and was one of the four elected. Bullock had other concerns. Not long after the new government began operating, he headed east, leaving Star to handle the store and to represent the partnership before the new city council.[11]

Bullock left Deadwood in October 1876 and would be gone for nearly five months. His primary goal was to visit his wife and daughter in Tecumseh, Michigan. While there, he decided to expand his family. His second daughter, Florence, would be born in October 1877. He also took time to further his political career. He corresponded with Governor John L. Pennington of Dakota Territory, urging that the Black Hills be removed from Indian control and that counties be organized as soon as possible. Pennington responded that steps had been taken to fulfill both of those objectives. In the process, Pennington and Bullock got to know each other, and the governor became aware of Bullock's political ambitions. Bullock also spent time in New York City, finding new merchandise for the store. In February, he wrote to Star explaining that he had purchased a variety of new goods, including cigars, tea, and whiskey, in anticipation of a business rush in the spring of 1877.[12]

While Bullock remained east, his hopes for the Black Hills came true. In February 1877, Congress imposed a treaty on the Indians, removing the region from the Great Sioux Reservation, and the Dakota territorial legislature created three counties: Lawrence, Pennington, and Custer. The legislation allowed for the appointment of county officers, including three county commissioners, a sheriff, a treasurer, and six other positions in each county. Elsewhere in Dakota, the governor only appointed three temporary commissioners for each new county, and they then held special elections to fill all positions locally. In the case of the Black Hills counties, however, the legislature saw the lawlessness and tumult of the gold camps as a threat to the process. They calculated that perhaps nine-tenths of the residents were not eligible to vote. The legislators consequently made all the positions appointive, with the understanding that they would serve until the next regularly scheduled election. While perhaps well-meaning, the legislation set off a furor among Black Hills inhabitants who worried about the loss of local control.[13]

Governor Pennington made his appointments in March, a few weeks after the counties were created, and while he pondered his selections, letters poured in, commenting on whom he should or should not appoint. For instance, one correspondent wrote that Sol Star should be appointed county commissioner, while another reported that Star was not a solid party man and was not supported by the majority of Republicans. Pennington, recognizing the seriousness of the task, tried to select men who had character and ability. In some instances, he chose people with strong Deadwood connections, such as Seth Bullock for sheriff. In other instances, the men came from Yankton, the territorial capital.

By this time Bullock and Pennington had developed a friendship, and as Bullock headed back to Deadwood, he stopped in Yankton, and the governor entrusted him with the executive documents announcing the new officers for Lawrence County.[14] Once the selections became public, the preponderance of Yankton people made many in Deadwood denounce them as carpetbaggers, and they did not spare Bullock. Because he had been gone for five months, after only living in Deadwood for two and one-half months, he also looked like an outsider, and since he carried the authorization papers, one observer called the new county government "the Bullock 'carpet bag regime.'"[15]

Political uncertainty reigned in Deadwood. The provisional city government disbanded as soon as the county was organized, but the governor delayed in appointing county officials, leaving Deadwood without governance for half a month. The editor of the Black Hills Daily Times damned the governor for this situation, charging that he had "criminally neglected" the region.[16] Then, as the governor's appointees arrived, local complaints reinvigorated a movement to create a new territory for the Black Hills region. Since late 1876, some people around Deadwood had been trumpeting the notion that the mineral region of Dakota Territory should be a separate territory. Some proposed the name El Dorado, but it soon changed to Lincoln. Meetings and calls for action became constant in April of 1877, and Star and Bullock played a part. At a convention held to organize Lincoln Territory on 21 April, Star sat on the executive committee, while Bullock organized a reception for delegates. But overall, Star and Bullock's efforts were minimal. A new territory did not offer them much advantage. Bullock already had a good relationship with the governor, and both men knew they could do well politically in Dakota Territory.[17]

Despite the complaints about carpetbaggers, Bullock was excited about becoming sheriff. Nevertheless, the fact that he was appointed and not elected, along with the fact that he was the first legally vested law officer in the gold camp, caused strong emotions to surface. Some people praised him, while others hated him, but he had little time to worry about his popularity. He needed to focus on establishing the sheriff's office and transitioning the community from lawlessness to order. It would not be easy. In the first place, the county commissioners had the right to choose Lawrence County's seat of government, and they initially met in Crook City, northeast of Deadwood. That selection meant that the sheriff's office should be in that town, something Bullock had not anticipated. But Deadwood's outraged citizens convinced the commissioners to move the county seat to their community. Second, while most of the provisional city officials had resigned when the county was formed, Con Stapleton, who served as city marshal, continued doing his job after Bullock arrived, causing confusion about who was in charge. It did not take Bullock long, however, to assert his position and take control of law enforcement.[18]

One of Bullock's first tasks was to organize his office. As a practical point, he located the sheriff's office in Star & Bullock Hardware, and the business's fireproof storeroom functioned as the jail. By establishing his office in the store, he could serve as sheriff while simultaneously helping Star run the operation. Bullock then needed to select his junior officers. Over time, he hired as many as eight deputies, with several of these living at other locations in Lawrence County, such as Central City and Crook City. He also organized the night watchmen, who checked for fire hazards and made nightly rounds to detect any suspicious blazes.[19]

Some of what Bullock had to do as sheriff could be seen as routine, at least for a frontier gold camp. He frequently investigated claims of burglary, theft, and embezzlement, and in one instance, he broke up a good-sized gang of outlaws who had been robbing mining claims and stores. When it came to everyday life, Bullock let most of the disagreements work themselves out, a fact that becomes evident when one considers that Deadwood had about sixty saloons and that Bullock seldom arrested anyone for drunk and disorderly conduct.[20] He did, however, break up the occasional street fight. In one instance, two men were engaged in what the newspaper called a "rough and tumble hand to hand knock down" on Main Street. As an audience of between two and three hundred people watched the show, Bullock and a deputy appeared. They promptly ended the fight, shackling the wrists and ankles of the two combatants.[21]

More serious problems for Bullock came from the fact that Deadwood was expanding. Although growth slowed during the winter of 1876–1877, Deadwood's population increased to around fifty-five hundred in the spring, nearly doubling the previous year's number. While that may have been good news for Star & Bullock Hardware, it meant that more people competed for the same opportunities. By 1877, all the valuable mineral ground and most of the preferred building sites for both businesses and residences had been taken. The scarcity of resources caused more competition and more violence. Where the Deadwood area had had about six non-Indian related homicides in 1876, this number increased to around eleven in 1877, many of which involved land and mineral disputes.[22]

Bullock encountered land-claim issues soon after becoming sheriff. In late March 1877, a group of men began constructing a building in a South Deadwood street, angering nearby residents. A crowd formed, and as raised voices turned to threats, the combatants pulled their guns. Bullock arrived just in time to prevent bloodshed. He promptly dispersed the crowd and took possession of the disputed land.[23] A few weeks later, another disagreement arose over a lot on Lee Street. This time the antagonists exchanged shots. Luckily, the bullets did not strike the participants or the "eager crowd of sight-seers" that had gathered. Bullock told the men, in his stern, low voice, to "subside," reminding them that the courts would decide property ownership.[24]

Bullock, however, did not always arrive in the nick of time. On the same day as the Lee Street affair in late April, a saloonkeeper named A. F. Chapman appeared in Bullock's office to report that a group of men were building a cabin on some land he had claimed the previous winter just above South Deadwood. He wanted the sheriff to get them off. Bullock responded that he could not and that only the courts could decide property claims. While Bullock deferred, John Blair (known as "Darby"), Samuel May (known as "Turkey Sam"), and a few others, mostly drifters from Chapman's bar, went to the site to remove the purported jumpers. They encountered a small number of men, which included Dan Obrodovich, working on a log cabin. When questioned about the land, Obrodovich and the other cabin builders professed innocence, saying that they had just recently arrived in camp and did not know the land had been claimed. Blair pointed his six-shooter at one of the interlopers and said, "If you want some of this I'll give it to you."[25] A rapid succession of pistol shots, perhaps as many as nine, soon followed. Obrodovich, hit twice, died while trying to retrieve his revolver, and two other cabin builders were wounded. None of Chapman's men suffered an injury.[26]

The gunfire brought Bullock running, along with many others in town. Quickly looking over the situation, the sheriff arrested May and Blair and led them off to jail. Oddly, he did not disarm the men. As they approached the jail, a deputy appeared and took their weapons. This oversight either speaks to Bullock's self-confidence or to his lack of training. Later, Bullock would also arrest Chapman as an accessory, and the three men went on trial for what the Black Hills Daily Times labeled the "Hill Homicide." The court found them guilty and the judge sentenced Blair and May to five years in jail for murder, while Chapman got fined twenty-five dollars for his role as an accessory.[27] While the sentences seem light for the crimes committed, these convictions were the first under the new legal authority of the county. According to one of Bullock's deputies, A. M. Willard, they provided a "good and wholesome lesson to the toughs and it gave them to understand that law and order would be enforced."[28]

Disagreements over mining claims were even more common than fights over building sites, and these disputes too often turned violent. Sometimes the event erupted so rapidly that Bullock or his deputies played no part, such as when John Bryant and A. W. Adams argued over a placer claim at the mouth of Sawpit Gulch, near Central City. When Bryant called Adams a liar, Adams pulled his pistol and fired, mortally wounding Bryant with a bullet just above the heart. Before he dropped, Bryant fired his gun three times at the fleeing Adams. One shot passed through Adams's brain, instantly killing him.[29]

Mineral disputes also went underground. In Hidden Treasure Gulch, also near Central City, the Aurora and Keets mining companies could not agree on the extent of their ore bodies. Each claimed ground that the other was mining, and they dug so close to each other that some of their tunnels interconnected. The owners of the two mines planned to have their case heard in court, but in the interim, they developed a compromise whereby both operations could continue working. Gold, however, does strange things, and each set of miners tried to get the upper hand. Finally, on the night of 4 September, forty armed men from the Keets mine used one of the connecting tunnels to enter the underground workings of the Aurora. Once inside, they blocked the Aurora's shaft. The next morning, one of the owners of the Aurora Mine, J. C. Tuttle, saw the barrier and set off a blast of powder to remove it. The explosion aroused the men, and the two companies soon began exchanging gunfire. Not to be deterred, Tuttle gathered a wheelbarrow to remove the debris from his blast, but as he bent over to grease the wheelbarrow's wheel, a bullet struck him in the back. He died soon after.[30]

The situation intensified after Tuttle's death. A group of men from the Aurora Mine surrounded the cabin on the Keets property, believing that the guilty party must be within. More violence could have erupted at any time, except that Bullock arrived on the scene. He rapidly took command, placing himself between the armed camps. Bullock suspected the Keets people of causing the trouble, and to make sure no more violence occurred, he arrested eight Keets men from inside the cabin, confiscating seven guns. Bullock, not yet satisfied, later arrested six more men, including the Keets superintendent, and took possession of the mine. The sheriff then refused to release the men on their own recognizance, keeping them out of circulation as long as possible. These actions caused the *Black Hills Daily Times* to praise Bullock for the "coolness, judgment and presence of mind he displayed at the time the arrest was made, when, to say the least, the situation had a critical appearance."[31] After a long trial, however, the jury could not agree on who killed Tuttle, and the case was dismissed.[32]

Beyond handling disputes over land and mineral claims, Bullock also had to deal with violence on the trails into Deadwood. The Cheyenne-Black Hills Stage Company began running stages to Deadwood in September 1876, and other stage lines soon followed. Since they traveled the trails alone, these coaches made attractive targets to outlaws. Sheriff Bullock also needed to be concerned about highwaymen taking refuge in Deadwood, no matter where along the trails they robbed a stage. Robbers found the rough frontier town a safe place to hide out and a good place to spend their ill-gotten gains.[33]

While most road agents preferred to rob stages as far away from settlements as possible, five Deadwood men decided to hold up the Cheyenne to Deadwood stage just two and one-half miles out of town, near the confluence of Gold Run and Whitewood creeks. Here the would-be robbers took their places, and as the stage approached, one yelled out: "Halt!" At this command, stage driver Johnny Slaughter attempted to stop the coach, but the team spooked. This unexpected reaction caused a man nicknamed Reddy (McKenna) to fire his sawed-off shotgun at Slaughter, blowing him off the stage and killing him instantly. The horses then bolted down the road, hurrying the stage toward Deadwood.[34]

The attempted robbery and murder caused an uproar, and Bullock immediately formed a posse to go to the scene of the crime, where they found Slaughter's body but no clues. The next day, Bullock began arresting suspicious characters, but a lack of evidence prevented him from holding anyone. Reddy, however, had left the Black Hills immediately after the crime. As the story implicating Reddy came out, people in Deadwood wanted him brought to justice. The stage company, Sheriff Bullock, and Governor Pennington offered awards for the arrest and conviction of Reddy and any other man involved in Slaughter's murder. Over the next eighteen months, Bullock made it his mission to bring Reddy to justice, ultimately tracking him to Ohio. Unfortunately for Bullock, Ohio had already convicted Reddy of multiple crimes and refused to turn him over.[35]

Most stage robberies happened farther away from Deadwood and the Black Hills. A favored location was the point at which the Cheyenne-Deadwood Trail crossed the Cheyenne River, a spot known as Robbers' Roost. But as outlaws drifted into Deadwood, some of their victims eventually recognized them. In August 1877, D. B. ("Boone") May spotted the three bandits who had held up his stage four weeks earlier. May went to Bullock, insisting that he arrest the men, but Bullock refused. With no evidence and conflicting accounts, Bullock argued that little could be accomplished. May then decided to confront the men himself. He approached Prescott Webb near the junction of Sherman and Lee streets, where the two exchanged shots. Both men were hit but kept firing until

Webb grabbed a nearby horse. As he mounted to make a getaway, he fired into the growing crowd of onlookers.

Bullock and two deputies ran toward the sound of the shots. One deputy shot Webb's horse, and Bullock and the other deputy, Captain Willard, approached the downed man. Webb lamented that he was done for, but as the lawmen got within a few feet, the outlaw drew his pistol and pulled the trigger twice. Fortunately for Bullock and Willard, the gun misfired. After sending the blood-soaked Webb to jail, Bullock and Willard captured his two associates. All three were ultimately sent to Cheyenne for trial, but all were acquitted.[36]

A few months later, Bullock saw a better opportunity to nab two road agents. The men, known as Blackburn and Wall, already had warrants against them, and they usually camped three miles outside of Crook City when not working the trails. A local rancher grew suspicious of the men, and he notified Bullock of their presence. Bullock brought two of his deputies from Deadwood to make the arrests, and they hid outside the camp in an attempt to surprise the outlaws. As Blackburn and Wall neared the stakeout, Bullock's gun accidentally discharged, and the two highwaymen leapt for cover. A gun battle ensued, with Blackburn suffering a wound, but he and Wall managed to escape. No doubt mortified, Bullock and his men determinedly chased the bandits for several days, but without success.[37] Bullock returned to Deadwood empty-handed, and his enemies used this event to label him as incompetent, accusing him of "dereliction of duty."[38]

While road agents and claim jumpers occupied Bullock's attention in 1877, the possibility of Indian attacks also remained strong. Deadwood seemed secure, but the Lakotas remained active on the edge of the Black Hills. In July, while a party of engineers with a military escort was surveying the border between Wyoming and Dakota territories, the

Indians attacked them in camp on the Belle Fourche River. When dramatically embellished reports of the incident reached Deadwood, the citizens went wild. Local agitators gave speeches, saying that the soldiers must be saved, and men from all walks of life volunteered to fight.[39]

Unfortunately, Bullock was out of town, chasing a horse thief, and none of his deputies effectively took charge of organizing the volunteers. While one went to the corrals and stables to appropriate the needed horses, others looked for arms and ammunition. Soon a group of fifty men left town, but according to the Black Hills Daily Times, they could not agree upon a commander. So, they decided to the let the fastest horseman lead, and a race ensued. Different leaders emerged as they pushed north of the Hills, with some pushing and shoving going on to gain advantage. During the jostling, one rider's gun went off, killing another man's horse. Once they arrived north of Spearfish, they found the soldiers alive, but three wagons and eighteen mules had been lost to the Indians. The volunteers fanned out to find the assailants, but they soon realized that the Lakotas had too much of a head start. Instead, the Deadwood group located the bodies of four white men along the Redwater River, ten miles north of Spearfish. Before the Indian threat ended, ten whites would be killed north of the Hills.[40]

Bullock arrived in town the day after the volunteers departed, and passions were still running high. The excitement had caused the county commissioners to offer a $250 bounty for an Indian, "dead or alive."[41] Having gotten a late start, Bullock responded vigorously. Instead of calling immediately for more volunteers, he telegraphed Governor Pennington that several ranchmen had already been killed and he wanted to gather another force of men but had no guns. Pennington responded the same day, relating that he had no weapons either but giving Bullock the authority to "organize one or more companies of militia under the laws of the Territory." He also promised to telegraph the secretary of war for assistance.[42]

Bullock called for five companies of militia cavalry, containing thirty men each. To find enough suitable riders, he divided the companies among Lawrence County towns, with two coming from Deadwood, one from Crook City, one from Spearfish, and one from Gayville. The members had to provide their own weapons and horses, and each company elected its own officers. The county commissioners were responsible for any expense that these men might incur, but the bill would then be passed on to the territorial and federal governments. By the time the militia was organized, however, troops had arrived from Fort Robinson in Nebraska and Fort Laramie in Wyoming. These forces brought quietude to the northern Black Hills, and the militia companies disbanded.[43]

When historian George W. Kingsbury wrote about these events in 1915, he claimed that Bullock's actions "prevented what in all probability would have resulted in a frontier war that would have cost many valuable lives with its attendant cost and destruction of property."[44] While Bullock's activities may have calmed jittery nerves among Lawrence County residents, it is an overstatement to say he stopped a frontier war. Nevertheless, such comments in the early twentieth century certainly added to what at that time was a growing Bullock legend.

Indian raids and frontier violence were characteristic of western gold camps, and Bullock had expected to deal with these events as sheriff. But late in 1877, he had to handle a wage-labor dispute at the Keets Mine that seemed to indicate a new era of post-frontier industrial mining. After the turmoil over the Tuttle murder had settled down, the Keets men got back to work. The loss of work time, however, had disrupted the cash flow, and the mining contractor, Joseph A. Conley, did not pay the men. Such occurrences often happened in gold-rush camps, and the unfortunate miners generally just walked away. Many early mining men were frustrated prospectors, looking for a little money so they could move on. Not getting paid meant that they had made a bad choice and needed to find a better job. The thirty or more men at the Keets Mine, however, had a different idea. They apparently came to the Black Hills with underground-mining experience, and they brought with them the idea of worker solidarity, which existed in other hardrock-mining regions. When they did not get paid, they took over the mine, staging an early version of a sit-down strike. Some would remain inside the mine from 6 through 22 November.[45]

Property owners had the sympathy of the law, and it fell to Bullock to remove the men from the mine. Reports have it that he tried a variety of tactics. He first "thundered threats down the air shaft," but to no avail.[46] He and his deputies then attempted a frontal assault, but the miners responded with "such an effective fusillade that the lawmen were sent scurrying."[47] He next tried to starve them out, but sympathizers on the surface kept sneaking food in to the strikers. After several failures, Bullock again thought of forcibly ejecting the men, but the workers had so many friends in the neighboring town of Central City, he feared violence would follow. Consequently, on 11 November, he wired Governor Pennington, requesting troops. The governor agreed, but the troops would not arrive until 21 November, causing a ten-day stalemate.[48]

When the fifty military men finally arrived, Bullock took more aggressive steps. With the army there to control any potential civil disorder, the sheriff informed the strikers that they needed to surrender, but they still refused. With the soldiers guarding the mine's perimeter, Bullock sealed off the mine's air shafts and sent burning sulfur down the main shaft. The noxious fumes soon filled the mine, and the stink caused the strikers to emerge, sputtering and choking.

Bullock promptly arrested them, and on the next day, 23 November, he returned the mine to its owners. His actions contributed to his reputation as a quick-thinking, no-nonsense lawman. Yet, he did have to call on the military for support, indicating some timidity when dealing with labor troubles and uneasiness in working-class communities. And while the use of burning sulfur became part of Bullock lore, his actions also made him the enemy of the area's mining population.[49]

As Bullock kept order in Lawrence County, he also dealt with two routine responsibilities that seemed to overwhelm his more dramatic activities. Travel in the line of duty was one, and he spent large amounts of time out of town, chasing road agents and horse thieves and taking prisoners to other jails. These travels sometimes kept him away at such critical moments as the Indian scare. The other obligation was tending to his constantly increasing jail population. He had no inmates in March 1877, but the number grew to eleven by July. With this influx, the county built a new eight-cell jail in South Deadwood, replacing Star and Bullock's fireproof. The prison population quickly outgrew this facility, as well. By October, it contained over forty men. The growing number of inmates and the cramped conditions led to repeated jailbreaks, but Bullock and his deputies managed to foil each one.[50]

By the end of 1877, Bullock had dealt with nearly every contingency imaginable during his nine months as sheriff, and while Deadwood residents often heard the echo of gunshots, little of that came from Bullock or his deputies. In fact, Lawrence County's first sheriff seldom needed his guns, and when he did, it was to arrest claim jumpers and road agents. Ironically, the saloon crowd caused few problems for Bullock. In fact, only one death in Deadwood in 1877 can be linked to a barroom dispute, and in that case, a night watchman shot and killed Peter Grant for pestering a "lady" outside the Bonanza Saloon.[51] But even as Bullock tried to bring order to the community, many in the county continually expressed dissatisfaction over how he and the other county officials had gotten their jobs, and the most outspoken planned to do something about it.

3

Struggling for Direction

While Bullock tended to his duties, many Lawrence County citizens fumed over the governor's choices for county officials. They not only perceived the appointees as outsiders, but worse, they feared that politicians in Yankton, known as the "Yankton ring," manipulated the imposed officers for their own benefit. As well, the issue of a permanent county seat had to be resolved. While the people in Deadwood had convinced the commissioners to meet in their city, neighboring towns hoped to lure them away. Some Deadwood residents wanted these issues settled, and during the summer of 1877, they circulated a petition demanding that the commissioners hold a special election.[1]

Other Deadwood residents took a different point of view, circulating a petition against a special election on the grounds that it would be illegal and against the wishes of the governor. These people, who included Sol Star, maintained that the appointments should stand until the next scheduled election in November 1878. Bullock did not sign this petition, probably because of his position as sheriff, but he obviously supported it. In part, he must have been conscious that not enough time had passed since his appointment for him to prove his ability and disassociate himself from Governor Pennington and the Yankton ring. He surely recognized, as well, that his association with the Republican party hurt his chances among the Democrat majority in Lawrence County. In other words, he feared he would lose a special election. The county commissioners agreed with this second petition and refused to call an election on the grounds that it would be illegal, might cause civil disorder, and would bring expensive litigation.[2]

Those who wanted the special election then took their case to the district federal judge, Granville Bennett. He ruled on 12 October 1877 that, although the governor may have wanted his appointees to serve until the next scheduled election, territorial law stated that the commissioners were obligated to call a special election. The decision mandated a vote during the first week of November, starting a flurry of political activity. The Democrats promptly organized a slate of candidates. The Republicans responded, but to compensate for their minority status, they nominated Democrats for a few offices and renamed themselves the "People's Party."[3] The sheriff's race, with Bullock running on the People's ticket, rapidly became the principal contest.

The prominence of the sheriff's office and Bullock's role as party spokesman caused his supporters and detractors alike to weigh in. Bullock's critics blasted him for dereliction of duty and incompetence, stemming from his failure to capture Blackburn and Wall and from his absence at the start of the recent Indian scare. They also claimed that he was dishonest, spending too much money on the construction of the county jail. The editor of the *Black Hills Daily Times* finessed the Crook City debacle by pointing to the wounding of the outlaws and stated that official business had kept Bullock away when the Indian problems arose.[4] The paper then highlighted his accomplishments, arguing that chaos prevailed before Bullock became sheriff and claiming that he brought "a security for life and property that, at his inauguration, seemed impossible to obtain. He has rid the country of bunko men, confidence operators, thieves, cut-throats and criminals generally."[5]

On 6 November, the voters chose Deadwood as the permanent county seat, but Bullock and most of the People's party candidates lost their bids for office. Certainly the Democratic majority hurt Bullock, as did his association with Governor Pennington, but his defeat could also be attributed to the background and personality of his opponent, John Manning. Like Bullock, Manning had once served as sheriff in Montana, and when he got to the northern Black Hills, he became involved in a variety of civic functions, such as the fire department. Beyond his qualifications, Manning also had the advantage of owning a saloon in Deadwood. At his establishment, he got to know the voters, and, as the *Times* reported with horror, he kept "a certain class of individuals full of liquor . . . to build up a reputation for generosity."[6]

Beyond experience and liberality, Manning had another advantage over Bullock. On a personal level, Bullock came across as detached and aloof. He did not relate well with the working class, who readily recognized that Bullock was not a laboring man. Vote totals reinforce this perception. Bullock lost in the towns with a majority of miners: Central City, Gayville, and Lead City. But he carried those locations with a more middle-class population dominated by merchants and where he had spent most of his time: Deadwood and Crook City.[7]

Like many frontier elections, this one probably had its share of fraud and "repeaters," but most likely the two sides canceled each other out. Some Black Hills historians, however, point to this election as especially corrupt, with Bullock leading the abuses. They claim that he arranged for soldiers from Fort Meade to dress in civilian clothes and vote repeatedly in Sturgis. Unfortunately for this story, Fort Meade and Sturgis were not established until 1878. Bullock was certainly not above trying to manipulate an election, but in 1877, he did not use soldiers to do his bidding.[8]

As soon as the election results were released, another dispute arose. The newly elected officials wanted to take their offices immediately, but the outgoing people refused to resign or vacate the county building. After one unsuccessful attempt to occupy the facilities, sheriff-elect Manning and a few others returned with a table and chairs and managed to occupy one of the building's rooms, proclaiming themselves the county's legal authority. The outgoing officeholders, however, denied it. They resisted the change in administration, not because they were angry, but because they thought their terms lasted until the first Monday in January 1878. Through November and December 1877, Deadwood had two county governments, including two sheriffs. They operated simultaneously, with each ignoring the other's decisions. During this period, Bullock retained the sheriff's records and control of the jail. In the meantime, Judge Bennett ruled locally in favor of the newly elected people, but Bullock and other defeated officeholders appealed the decision to the territorial Supreme Court. The court quickly reviewed the case and agreed with Bennett. With this decision, Bullock turned the jail and the sheriff's records over to Manning, ending his nine and a half months as Lawrence County's first sheriff on 28 December, one week before he planned.[9]

Bullock had become sheriff at a difficult time in Lawrence County's history. Violence and crime increased as the area grew, and the cases mentioned do not include all that Bullock had to deal with. For instance, the Chinese woman Di Lee was savagely murdered in November 1877. While Bullock certainly investigated, no culprits could be found. Sheriff Bullock wanted to end these murders and bring law and order to Deadwood, and by some accounts, he succeeded. If homicides, however, are used as a measuring stick, Bullock, in fact, did not "clean up" the city. And murders would continue to plague the town, with perhaps as many as fifteen in 1878, advancing from the eleven during 1877. This increase certainly indicates that major crime still existed in town, but it might also imply that Sheriff Manning was not as capable as Bullock. If that was the case, however, the voters of Lawrence County had a chance to remove Manning from office in the election of 1878, when they reelected him for another term. The murder rate dropped by nearly fifty percent the following year. What the data probably show is the maturation of a frontier gold camp. Locations such as Deadwood had unstable, violent periods when the criminal element flocked in, but within a few years, most outlaws had either left or settled down.[10]

Bullock's role in early Deadwood, however, should not be underestimated. As the first sheriff, he laid the foundation for law and order, and he demonstrated that there would be consequences for bad behavior. It just took the outlaws time to realize that. His stint as sheriff also brought fame for himself. All in Lawrence County knew him. While not all liked him, he gained the respect and friendship of the propertied and the elite. For instance, Judge Bennett, although he had ruled against the outgoing administration, saw Bullock as a diligent enforcer of the law, and he considered Bullock the standard by which all other sheriffs should be measured.[11]

Even though Bullock won some acclaim, he probably did not realize that his time as sheriff would be a defining period in his life. As Deadwood aged and the frontier faded, more Americans started reminiscing about the bygone Wild West days and what the frontier meant to the development of the national character. Americans attended entertainments, such as Buffalo Bill's Wild West Show, that dramatized western events. As William F. ("Buffalo Bill") Cody's "Deadwood Coach" circled the nation's show arenas, Deadwood won a place in the American imagination. Some of the curious heard about Bullock's exploits as the town's first sheriff, and as his notoriety rose, he began to play the part. By the early twentieth century, Bullock was more than willing to tell stories about his early days in Deadwood, embellishing them where he thought appropriate.[12]

Bullock's legacy, however, did not create the same level

of interest, nor did it have the longevity, of some other west-ern folk-heroes, such as Wild Bill Hickok and Wyatt Earp. In part, Bullock's story did not contain the requisite amount of bloodshed. He had not participated in shoot-outs in the street like Wild Bill, and he did not have a Deadwood ver-sion of the O.K. Corral. In fact, he did not kill anyone while in Deadwood, and few accounts show him even firing his gun. He did not die a martyr's death, such as Wild Bill did in a Deadwood bar. Unlike Calamity Jane, Bullock did not become the star of dime novels, which immortalized her marginal achievements.[13] Finally, he was Deadwood's sher-iff for less than ten months, providing little material for a lasting legacy. Although his national fame did not endure, within the Black Hills, Bullock is still closely identified with the law and order he first worked to establish there.

And despite leaving the sheriff's office in 1877, Bullock's career in law enforcement was not over. In September 1877, while Bullock still worked as sheriff, the United States mar-shal for Dakota Territory, John B. Raymond, had appointed him as one of five deputy marshals for the territory. Many United States marshals in western territories selected county sheriffs for their deputies because these officers already knew the lay of the land and the local criminal ele-ment. And they often needed extra money. Their duties were to support the federal courts and to enforce federal laws. Deputies were generally paid on a fee basis, collecting a set amount for each task accomplished. Bullock served sum-monses for grand juries, enforced federal liquor laws, and investigated counterfeiting rings. In some instances, he worked with Sheriff Manning, searching for stage robbers and fugitives. Bullock served as deputy marshal until prob-ably 1886, and he undoubtedly fulfilled his assignments, but he does not appear to have put much effort into them. His record is relatively sparse for his nine years of service, and it may have been that the fee schedule did not make the job attractive. Or, Bullock may have found other activities more fulfilling.[14]

One incident, however, did attract Bullock's attention. On 26 September 1878, the Black Hills treasure coach, named the Johnny Slaughter after the fallen stage driver, was robbed at Canyon Springs on the Cheyenne trail, thirty-six miles south of Deadwood. John ("Jack") Gilmer and Monroe Salisbury, who operated the Cheyenne-to-Deadwood stage line, built the treasure coach to carry gold bullion and other valuables out of the area. It featured iron plating and a safe that would reportedly take robbers twenty-four hours to open. The special stage made weekly trips, generally accompanied by three to six guards. Locals sometimes referred to the coach as the Monitor, after the ironclad Civil War ship.

On this September day, the safe carried over twenty-five thousand dollars in gold dust, bars, and jewelry. Three guards and one passenger accompanied the driver and the stage's precious cargo. At the remote Canyon Springs station, six gunmen had tied up the station tender and lay in wait. As the coach arrived, they opened fire, and an exchange of shots followed. The holdup men wounded two guards and killed the passenger, while the guards killed one holdup man and wounded another. But the highwaymen gained the upper hand and took control of the stage. After two more hours, they cracked the safe and left with the contents.[15]

Word spread rapidly to Deadwood, and the usual wave of excitement swept through town. Some men formed a volunteer troop and dashed out of town to hunt the robbers. A number of other people rushed to the scene of the crime just to satisfy their curiosities. Bullock did not join in the stampede, and according to his own recollections twenty-four years after the fact, he soon received a visit from Jack Gilmer, one of the stage company's owners. Gilmer, who valued Bullock's experience, asked the former sheriff what should be done. In response, Bullock told Gilmer the obvious: pursue the attackers wherever they may lead and capture them. Gilmer then asked Bullock to do just that, but Bullock demurred, saying he had no official position and was too busy managing his hardware business. Gilmer insisted, offering Bullock "carte blanche," meaning he could take "any and all horses" from his stage stations, and he sweetened the deal with a reward.[16] Bullock finally agreed. He recruited six men, including a division superintendent for the stage line, and they set off for the scene of the crime. Why Bullock claimed that he had no authority is unclear; maybe he wished to emphasize his own importance when he told the story, but as the local Democratic newspaper pointed out at the time, Bullock went after the robbers because he was the "deputy U. S. marshal."[17]

For the next seven days, Bullock and his men pursued the villains, following their trail south and east through the Black Hills. Bullock's troop passed Newton's Fork near Hill City, stopped briefly at the gold camp of Sheridan, and went on to Rapid City. Once there, they encountered a second group, which included Ed Cook, another superintendent from Gilmer's stage line, and the sheriff of Pennington County. Bullock anticipated that Cook would provide him with fresh horses, but instead, Cook's party joined the pursuit, much to Bullock's dismay. Bullock needed the new horses. His were tired, and he did not know how much farther the animals could carry his group, but they kept on the trail.

Bullock's and Cook's posses headed east, and near Fort Pierre, they encountered a camp that they believed contained the suspects. At this point, Bullock wanted to attack, but Cook said that they should wait until morning. After some agitated discussion, Cook prevailed. When morning came, the highwaymen were gone. This calamity caused Bullock and his men to give up. After traveling seven hundred miles in seven days, they and their horses were exhausted. For all their effort, Bullock's party accomplished nothing and rode away frustrated. Over time, other lawmen would capture the thieves and recover the majority of the treasure.[18] Bullock's failure allowed his enemies to challenge his competence once again. But this event, which is the most famous stage robbery in Black Hills history, could have had the opposite effect. If Bullock had succeeded in capturing the robbers and reclaiming the treasure, it could have elevated him to western legend status. But, that did not happen.

Beyond serving as deputy marshal, Bullock remained active in other civic affairs. Beginning in April 1878, he decided to reinvigorate the Deadwood fire department. Bullock had always had an interest in fire control. He served as chief engineer for the Helena fire department, and his duties with the Board of Health and Street Commissioners in Deadwood included serving as a fire warden. Once he became sheriff, he also controlled the night watchmen as they checked for fires, but the responsibility to organize a fire department fell outside of the county government's purview. A group of Deadwood citizens, which did not include Bullock, had formed a hook-and-ladder company in June 1877 and acquired a hose cart soon after. But interest waned, and when a snowstorm collapsed the roof of their building in March 1878, they quit meeting.[19] Soon after, the *Black Hills Daily Times* editorialized that nothing will be done until a "sweeping conflagration . . . will wipe out our city of Deadwood."[20]

Bullock developed a plan to correct this deficiency, but when the ex-sheriff came up with ideas, they were seldom small ones. In this case, Bullock reasoned that the community would only support a fire department if it had the best equipment, could be a source of pride, and served a social function. To get top-notch equipment, Bullock began soliciting funds to purchase a fire engine that pumped water via a steam engine. Most other fire departments pumped water by hand, but Bullock had seen a steam-powered fire engine operate in Helena, and he believed Deadwood needed one. Stimulated by Bullock's drive for a new engine, forty men formed a fire department, promptly electing Bullock foreman (over Sheriff John Manning). To instill pride among his recruits, Bullock established a committee to select uniforms. The design included red flannel shirts with a crossed hook and ladder on the front. To develop the social aspects of the group, the members planned a firemen's ball in conjunction with the Fourth of July celebration. By the summer of 1878, the fire department had sixty-nine volunteers and three different companies: hose, hook-and-ladder, and engine.[21]

Just as rapidly as interest developed, it began to fade. By September, the newspaper called for the fire companies' foremen to meet more regularly and build enthusiasm among the men. Part of the failing can be blamed on Bullock. He had been the driving force, but other responsibilities diverted his attention. For instance, he had to leave town frequently. As deputy marshal, he was gone for a week while chasing the bandits from the Canyon Springs affair, and he spent considerable time in Ohio, trying to bring murderer Reddy McKenna back to Deadwood for trial. Also, he traveled to Michigan in July to retrieve his wife and daughters. Once he got his family to town, establishing a home became a higher priority than leading a fire department.[22]

Bullock also let the fire department slide because, when it came to civic projects, Bullock had one defining pattern: he often gave the initial push, but then he let the project go. He wanted someone else to follow through and do the day-to-day work to make the endeavor succeed. If new leadership did not step forward, then the undertaking would falter, as was the case with the fire department. Bullock always saw himself as a leader, but when it came to civic endeavors, he was only the idea man.

As the fire department floundered, all aspects of its operation came under review. Some people questioned the value of the steam fire engine, claiming that few wanted it in the first place and that none wanted it once it arrived. Others pointed out that Deadwood did not have an adequate water source to fight a fire in the first place. In response, another campaign developed to dig more wells and build cisterns, but the necessary funds could not be found. Repeated efforts to do something brought just more talk, and many resolved to do what they could to prevent fire or to stop it from spreading on their own. Star and Bullock placed water-filled barrels on the roof of their building, hoping that the contents could extinguish any fire that might occur on the premises. By September 1879, another plan was put forward to buy hose, carts, and other necessary fire equipment, but the call came too late. Just weeks later, a fire would destroy most of Deadwood.[23]

Some of Bullock's public activities, such as promoting a fire department, may have been calculated, for he wanted to run for sheriff again in the regularly scheduled election of November 1878. In this campaign, the Lawrence County Republicans dropped the People's party title and competed as Republicans, with Bullock taking the lead.[24] During the summer of 1878, he attended party conventions in Deadwood and Yankton, and the Yankton newspaper praised him as "the leading and moving spirit in the republican delegation from his county and his successful management evinced a skill which is the product only of keen perception and a well balanced intellect."[25]

Bullock gained the nomination for sheriff at the Lawrence County Republican convention, while John Manning would again be his opponent. The editor of the Black Hills Daily Times quickly labeled this race the "chief contest" in the campaign and entered the fray on behalf of the Republicans. The paper attacked Manning, claiming that his office expenses had been too high, and it praised Bullock, saying that he would be an "honest disburser of the county funds."[26] The paper also described Bullock as "an honorable business man of many years experience, cool and self-possessed under the most trying circumstances."[27] When Bullock accepted the nomination, his greatest concern was how voters perceived him in relation to his competition. To counter Manning's image as a friend of the working class, Bullock promised that he would "enforce the law without regard to difference in wealth or position."[28]

Despite his best effort, Bullock lost again. While he won the majority of votes in the Deadwood area, Manning soundly defeated him in Central City and Gayville. The people there undoubtedly remembered Bullock's anti-union actions in the Keets Mine strike. This event had permanently branded him an enemy of the workingman. In this election, the new camp of Sturgis also weighed in, with the vote going strongly for Manning. The Black Hills Daily Times claimed fraud, stating that "transient soldiers and bull whackers" had voted in Sturgis without being residents.[29] What some early historians thought had happened in 1877 apparently did happen in 1878, but not in Bullock's favor. No matter the reason for his loss, it demoralized Bullock. A divide separated him from the region's many miners, and he did not know how to bridge it. He remained popular among businessmen, but he recognized that winning another major election would be virtually impossible. He would remain active in the Republican party, and his partner Sol Star would run for office, but Bullock himself would never again challenge for an elective position.

While the election results were disappointing, the newspaper coverage signaled the fact that the Star and Bullock partnership was a successful enterprise. Star still served as the primary partner, and the store's advertisements reflected his importance. While the Star and Bullock logo appeared at the top of their newspaper ads, Sol Star's full name appeared more prominently in the body of the advertisement. After Bullock left the sheriff's office, he became more involved in the everyday business of the store, and this attention allowed Star to leave town from time to time. Yet, Bullock disliked the confinement of the store. On one occasion, the newspaper commented that Bullock had "actually lost flesh" since Star had left him in charge.[30] Of course, the two partners employed a number of men in their business, but in Deadwood's early years, Bullock or Star generally felt obliged to supervise the day-to-day operations.[31]

The partners' enterprise did well in Deadwood because the two men responded to the changing needs and wants of their clientele. As the mining camp matured, they brought in new merchandise and expanded their activities. To their initial offering of mining supplies, they soon added glassware and queensware pottery from London, followed in a year or two by a variety of other household goods, such as flowerpots and wallpaper. In 1879, they put on display what the newspaper described as a solid silver tea set, causing the reporter to speculate on where they might find millionaires to buy it. The partners also began promoting farm implements. As the Indian raids diminished north of the Black Hills, farming increased, and Bullock wanted to capitalize on what he considered an essential endeavor for Deadwood's economic diversification and long-term prosperity. To this end, the two men sold plows, reapers, mowers, and anything else a farmer might want. Star also began taking on small construction jobs, such as putting a culvert in Main Street and placing shutters on the courthouse. All these new activities required larger quarters, and the partners not only expanded their Main Street location, but in 1878, they built a warehouse in South Deadwood.[32]

Bullock and Star also used political connections to increase their business. Star had allies in Washington, D.C., who put his name forward as Deadwood's next postmaster, a position that required a presidential appointment. In

May 1879, President Rutherford B. Hayes obliged. Star not only gained the financial benefit of a government job, but he operated the post office in conjunction with Star and Bullock Hardware, anticipating a business boom. In fact, all businessmen on lower Main Street saw an advantage in locating the post office there, and they contributed money to Star and Bullock so that they could secure the neighboring building for the needed expansion. When Star's commission began, the two men set up the post office in the old Star and Bullock Hardware building on the corner of Main and Wall, and relocated their business into the recently acquired structure next door. Star served as postmaster until a controversy over mail routes into Deadwood forced him out of office in late 1881.[33]

Even as Star and Bullock expanded their Deadwood business, the two men explored opportunities beyond the town. Living in a mining region, the partners naturally considered mineral investments. In their first years in Deadwood, they invested in at least two hardrock claims, but neither produced any gold. Bullock and Star also looked to agriculture as a way to diversify their holdings. Working through employees, the partners acquired 160 acres along upper False Bottom Creek, just north of the Hills, in 1878. Then as more settlers made claims in that area, they looked farther north, occupying additional land near the confluence of the Belle Fourche and Redwater rivers in 1879. Working with W. P. Tyler, Bullock and Star initially established a dairy farm, but they soon became ranchers, raising cattle and horses at what was variously known as the S & B Ranch, S & B Outfit, or the S & B Stock Farm.[34]

With expanding investments in and out of Deadwood, Bullock and Star could anticipate the arrival of the next decade with optimism, but there were some ominous signs. By late 1879, the placer claims along Whitewood and Deadwood creeks had nearly played out. Placer miners began leaving their claims, and their departure created an economic void in Deadwood. The northern Hills continued to produce gold, but it came mostly from hardrock mines, especially those located on the Homestake ore body that stretched from Central City to Lead City, three miles from Deadwood. While hundreds of miners worked there, they did not live in Deadwood, and most did not shop in Deadwood. While the distance between the towns was not great, travel was limited, in part because all roads to Deadwood were toll roads. The drop in business may have been what encouraged the partners to diversify their activities.[35]

As Bullock and Star pursued economic security, disaster struck. In the early morning hours of 26 September 1879, a fire broke out in a bakery on Sherman Street. It spread rapidly, hitting a hardware store where eight kegs of blasting powder exploded, showering Lee Street and beyond with burning debris. The fire soon went down Main Street and then up the hills to the residential areas, leveling almost everything in its path. People scrambled to the higher hills for safety, carrying whatever they could. In the end, only two small residential neighborhoods survived, as an estimated one hundred businesses and seventy-five dwellings were lost, at a value of nearly one and a half million dollars. The fire spread so quickly that little effort was made to put it out, exacerbated by the fact that the inferno destroyed most of the fire equipment. Bullock's steam fire engine survived, but it sat unused. As for Bullock and Star, they lost most of their business assets, at an estimated worth of about twenty thousand dollars. But their fireproof endured. As Bullock surveyed the ruined town, he labeled 26 September "Black Friday," and all in Deadwood agreed.[36]

The fire destroyed all remnants of gold-rush Deadwood, and it could have doomed the town itself. From the time of Bullock's arrival, doomsayers had doubted Deadwood's permanence. Once the placer gold played out, they predicted, the residents would move to towns based on hardrock mining, such as Lead City and Central City. Some of these same pessimists also argued that Deadwood Gulch was too narrow and too inconvenient to support a substantial community. And while some people left after the fire, believing that the end had come, Bullock and Star stayed. They had much to keep them in town. Since their arrival in 1876, they had acquired a substantial amount of property and gained a solid reputation as businessmen. Despite the fire, their recent diversification into ranching and mail-handling ensured some stability, no matter what happened in Deadwood. In addition, they reportedly had thirteen thousand dollars in insurance money to help them rebuild.[37]

Bullock and Star may also have realized that there were no more opportunities like Deadwood. First in Montana and then in the Black Hills, the two men had sought the economic and political advantages that came from frontier gold camps. While other gold rushes would occur after the Black Hills, none provided the same frontier experience. The people who came to the Black Hills found an area still under the control of the Indians, without white settlement, and beyond federal control. The early arrivals found themselves hundreds of miles from rail connections and isolated from the rest of the country, with violence as an integral part of getting to and living in the gold region. These characteristics had attracted Bullock and Star. In this environment, they expected to make good money and fulfill their political ambitions. In 1879, however, the two men must have realized that the nation's gold frontier had closed. Consequently, Deadwood would be their last stop. Bullock and Star, and Deadwood itself, would need to adapt to new circumstances and to a new era in order to survive.[38]

Seth Bullock began his career in public service as a volunteer fireman in Helena, Montana. Shown in this 1875 photograph are, from left to right, A. J. Davidson, C. N. Jeffers, Seth Bullock, and T. H. Kleinschmidt. Photograph by E. H. Train. Montana Historical Society, Helena

Bullock opened Deadwood's Star and Bullock Hardware
with Solomon ("Sol") Star in 1876. The store closed in 1900.
Adams Museum, Deadwood, S.Dak.

Sol Star 13th Pres Black Hill Pioneers
1/29/1916 J. C. H. Grabill, Photographer.
Term

A native of Bavaria, Sol Star was Seth Bullock's partner in
many business ventures. He also served as mayor of Deadwood.
Adams Museum, Deadwood, S.Dak.

Martha Eccles Bullock, Seth's childhood sweetheart, was active in music
and educational activities in Deadwood, where she raised three children.
Adams Museum, Deadwood, S.Dak.

The Merchants' National Bank building presented a grand appearance when it was constructed in 1880. Adams Museum, Deadwood, S.Dak.

The founders of Minnesela gathered at the Minnesela hotel around 1890. When the railroad bypassed the town and nearby Belle Fourche became the county seat, Minnesela became a ghost town. South Dakota State Historical Society

The main street of Belle Fourche boasted several
buildings with more under construction in the early 1890s.
South Dakota State Historical Society

The Bullock Hotel fulfilled the need for a first-class hotel in Deadwood when it opened in 1896. City of Deadwood

Dressed in chaps and bandanas
and sporting their pistols, a group
of Black Hills cowboys, led by Seth Bullock,
(front row, center) rode in Theodore
Roosevelt's inaugural parade in 1905.
Adams Museum, Deadwood, S.Dak.

CAPTAIN
SETH BULLOCK'S
COWBOYS

INAUGURATION OF
THEODORE ROOSEVELT

WASHINGTON,
1905

A ribbon topped
with a photograph
of Seth Bullock
commemorates the
1905 inaugural.
South Dakota State
Historical Society

In 1905, President Theodore Roosevelt appointed
Seth Bullock to a committee to revise the Forest
Service rule book. Bullock, second from the left in the
first row, is seated next to Gifford Pinchot, who, as
chief forester, occupies the ornate chair. Library of
Congress

The plaque text reads:

IN ME[MORY]
THEODOR[E]
"THE A[...]"
OCTOBER 27, 185[...]

THI[S]
IS ERECTED [...]
BLACK H[...]
JUl[...]

WHEREAS, [...]
SOCIETY OF PEACE [...]
[...]
[...]
[...]
LIFE AND ADVOCA[...]
WORTHY OF EMUL[A...]
HIS COUNTRYMEN,
RESOLVED BY T[...]
IN PERPETUATIO[N...]
HIS INDOMITABLE [...]
MOUNT[...]
TO ITS HOPE AN[...]

In one of the last photographs of his life, Seth Bullock stood near
the Black Hills monument to Theodore Roosevelt, which was dedicated
on 4 July 1919. Bullock died less than three months later.
South Dakota State Historical Society

Located among the pine trees at a site high above Deadwood, this unadorned tombstone marks the graves of Seth and Martha Bullock. Photograph by Michael Runge. Deadwood Historic Preservation Commission, Deadwood, S.Dak.

PROMOTER, SPECULATOR, AND DEVELOPER
1879–1895

4

Building upon the Ashes

As fire swept through Deadwood the night of 26 September 1879, the frightened residents rushed to the hills above, and from there they watched their town burn. Among them was Richard F. Pettigrew, a future United States senator from South Dakota. Years later, he recalled that as the blaze neared a building, the heat drew the sap out of the green lumber, as if priming the wood for fire, and once the blaze struck, it instantly engulfed the building. As it spread from structure to structure, the "fire made short work of Deadwood," Pettigrew observed. The next morning, Deadwood rose from the ashes. Walking through the devastation, Pettigrew saw businesses already reopening and reconstruction underway. In particular, he watched John Manning, who had stored his liquor in a mountainside warehouse, placing boards on barrels and hawking his wares. By eleven in the morning, drunks and card players had reclaimed Deadwood as their own.[1]

Tents and randomly built structures quickly went up everywhere. One block from Manning's improvised saloon, Star and Bullock began reconstructing their business. The fireproof had survived, and they immediately began selling their stored merchandise. At the rear of the fireproof, they erected what the newspaper called a "tin shop," employing six men to manufacture whatever people needed, such as doors and shutters. Bullock and Star hired more men to construct a storefront and a post office on Main Street. They planned to build with brick in the spring, but in the meantime, they wanted something for immediate use, which meant using wood. Unfortunately, the workmen built too rapidly, and high winds blew in the sides. Not discouraged, the two men again rebuilt.[2]

With the town in ruins, the residents needed help. County officials provided law enforcement, but Deadwood lacked a municipal government to aid in rebuilding the infrastructure and to deal with civic issues. To fill this void, residents created a "citizens' committee," and at this difficult time, the townspeople once more turned to Bullock for help, selecting him as one of six committee members. The Citizens' Committee lacked any real authority, and its decisions could have been easily ignored. But when the editor of the Black Hills Daily Times reflected on the fire's aftermath a month later, he reported, "All matters were referred [to the committee members], and their decisions [were], we are pleased to state, generally obeyed."[3]

The Times did not detail the committee's work but did comment on their search for "lost goods." The committee published a notice stating that a large amount of merchandise, household goods, and wearing apparel had disappeared in advance of the fire. The goods were "stored in Central and Lead cities, and in cabins along the roads leading to those places," the Times explained, adding that the items were probably "only misplaced, and in due time will be returned to their rightful owners." To facilitate this transaction, however, and perhaps to limit the suspicion of theft, the Citizens' Committee asked that the items be turned over to them for distribution to the rightful owners.[4] The success or failure of this endeavor went unrecorded.

The committee also tried to bring some permanent changes to Deadwood, but not all their efforts were successful. For instance, they sought to connect Sherman Street directly with Main Street. As it existed before the fire, Sherman Street, which had become the primary artery through South Deadwood, dead-ended at Wall Street, almost opposite Bullock and Star's business. If Sherman Street continued across the creek, it would eventually angle into Main Street. Bullock thought the fire provided the perfect opportunity to connect the two thoroughfares. Affected property owners, however, would not surrender the necessary easements, and the idea died.[5]

The committee also talked about organizing a permanent city government. Bullock and his fellow committee members saw incorporation as essential. A city government could provide better fire control and more effective governance. Its establishment could also give Deadwood the appearance of a growing, prosperous community, which seemed essential as the town strove to emerge from the devastation. The proposal did not go far in 1879, but the committeemen had planted a seed, and over the next two years, activists brought the idea before Deadwood voters three times. Despite losing all three elections, the supporters managed to convince the territorial legislature to incorporate Deadwood in February 1881. With incorporation, Deadwood took another step in shedding its boomtown past.[6]

The rapid reconstruction and the move for incorporation did not convince everyone that Deadwood had a future. For example, James McPherson, who had worked with James K. P. Miller, left soon after the fire. He, like many others, were attracted to the booming silver camps of Colorado, especially the town of Leadville.[7] The out-migration had begun even before the fire, but the conflagration increased the flow. The editor of the Black Hills Daily Times took notice of this trend and tried to discourage it. For instance, the newspaper reported that Leadville had "six feet of snow and an army of paupers clamoring for work or bread."[8] The departures continued, however, taking their toll. Where an estimated fifty-five hundred people lived in Deadwood in 1877, the census taker found just under thirty-eight hundred in 1880, and this number fell to about seventeen hundred in 1885.[9] If this pattern continued, Deadwood would eventually become another western ghost town.

Bullock and Star, recognizing that Deadwood needed new industries and new businesses to survive, took the lead by expanding their own ventures. The partners enlarged their hardware store and their ranch, and in each case, Bullock directed the expansion. The two men took on new roles, as well, with Bullock becoming active in banking and mining. In the process of trying to build a new Deadwood and make money for himself, Bullock became a promoter and a speculator. He took chances that easily equaled those he had taken when he first came to Deadwood, but without risking his life as he had as a lawman in 1876 and 1877. Instead, he gambled with his economic future. The 1880s would be Bullock's era of speculation. During this time, he would try to balance multiple endeavors simultaneously, and his business acumen would be severely tested. Yet, Bullock remained supremely confident that he could make all succeed.

Star and Bullock Hardware remained the center of Bullock's business world. By the spring of 1880, the post office and store had been reconstructed at the corner of Main and Wall streets. Behind these structures sat Bullock and Star's original fireproof, but laborers soon removed that building. In its place, stonemasons laid a large sandstone foundation, measuring nearly one hundred feet by fifty feet. On top of that they erected a one-story brick edifice, with metal doors and shutters. Inside, Bullock and Star located their warehouse and "the finest private office in town."[10] No matter what other businesses Bullock entered into during the 1880s, he used this location as his primary office. Built to be fireproof, the brick structure did its job well. When another blaze destroyed the wooden building fronts in 1894, the brick warehouse survived, and it still stands today.[11]

Corresponding with a new era and a rebuilt store, Star and Bullock Hardware began offering an even greater variety of merchandise. They continued to carry a wide array of household items, including paint and window glass, but to this inventory they added more farm equipment. To highlight the region's possibilities, bundles of rye and wheat decorated Bullock and Star's store windows during harvest season, and the partners sent barley and wheat samples to the Nebraska State Fair in 1881. At a location they owned near the corner of Sherman and Charles streets, the men sold wagons and buggies, and by 1884, the newspaper estimated their inventory to be worth seventy-five thousand dollars. In addition to sales, they continued bidding on small construction jobs, such as repairing roofs, and they enticed several of the local stage lines, including the coach to Spearfish, to make the hardware store their station stop. Business expanded enough for the pair to employ a full-time manager, hiring Fred Eccles, Bullock's brother in-law.[12]

Bullock's foray into more speculative ventures began when he established Star and Bullock hardware stores throughout the region. In March 1880, he opened one in Rapid City, followed in September with one in Spearfish. Neither town had many people. Rapid City had less than three hundred and Spearfish less than two hundred, but that did not concern Bullock. He planned to sell farm equipment to settlers along Rapid and Spearfish creeks in order to profit from the future prosperity of farming in the Black Hills. Anecdotal evidence indicates that he succeeded, at least initially. For instance, the Spearfish Register reported that Star and Bullock Hardware in Spearfish sold four steam-threshing machines in the early months of 1881.[13]

Over the next six years, Bullock continued to open businesses. As the Northern Pacific Railroad built through Montana in 1882, he established hardware stores in the new railroad towns of Billings and Miles City. These operations were followed with shops at Sturgis and Custer in the Black Hills and at Sundance, Wyoming. When the towns of DeMores (north of the Hills) and Carbonate (northwest of Deadwood) were created in 1885 and 1886, respectively, Bullock opened enterprises there, as well. At each of these locations, Bullock and Star joined with a new partner. This person shared the risk and managed the store. For example, John Eccles, another Bullock brother-in-law, ran the Sturgis store. Not all of these businesses lasted long, however. Bullock and Star closed the unprofitable ones and sold others to their partners. By 1887, the two men still had ties with five of the eight original branch operations: Custer, Spearfish, Sturgis, DeMores, and Carbonate. While smaller than the original Deadwood store, these satellites expanded Bullock and Star's business reach. They also extended their financial risks.[14]

Along with advancing their hardware operations, Bullock and Star expanded the S & B Ranch. With Bullock again setting the course, the partners dramatically increased their holdings. They initially held land at two locations, near False Bottom Creek and on the Belle Fourche River, but most of their new acquisitions came along the Belle Fourche River. They acquired land in this area, in part, because settlers had not yet moved in. Sitting thirteen miles north of the Black Hills, the Belle Fourche River was too remote from the local farm markets to encourage development. The land around False Bottom Creek, just north of the Black Hills, however, had already attracted several farmers by 1880.

The two men knew they had to act fast to protect what they wanted. A settler named Dominic Perrolio (also Dominique Peirroglia) had already occupied some of the land they sought. In late 1880, Bullock and Star purchased Perrolio's 160 acres, paying him two hundred dollars for his acreage and his interest in an irrigation ditch. While they desired the land, the water right was a bonus, and Bullock soon understood the value of irrigation in this semiarid environment. Ironically, Perrolio did not have legal title to the land he sold.

Like many settlers, he had squatted on the land, anticipating later ownership. He would not acquire that from the federal government until 1882 and then pass it along to Bullock and Star. In 1880, Bullock and Star did not worry about such federal niceties, they just wanted Perrolio's farm. By the next year, the partners controlled a total of 480 acres at the confluence of the Belle Fourche and Redwater rivers, slightly northeast of present-day Belle Fourche. They also held 160 acres on upper False Bottom Creek, where the Spearfish airport sits today.[15]

As they expanded their holdings, Bullock and Star had to watch for threats to their interests. For one, cattlemen were placing more animals on the open range north of the Belle Fourche River, enough cattle for stockmen to hold their first roundup in 1881. Cattle owners initially gave little thought to buying land. Once they placed a herd on the grasslands, they established a proprietary right to that area, and other cattlemen generally respected it. These new arrivals did not intentionally intrude upon Bullock's holdings, but open-range cattle occasionally did. Because Bullock and Star's land sat along the banks of the Belle Fourche River, thirsty animals wanted its grass and water, especially during dry years. While some observers estimated about one hundred thousand cattle in the entire Black Hills region in 1880, this number advanced to around five hundred thousand by 1884, with much of this increase coming to the range north of the Belle Fourche River. As the numbers grew, cattlemen bought property along the river to guarantee a place on the range. Bullock and Star needed to make sure that these expanding operations did not overwhelm the S & B Ranch.[16]

Another potential menace to Bullock and Star's holdings came from the new town of Minnesela. Three entrepreneurs, Ed M. Bowman, Azby A. Chouteau, and Dave T. Harrison, established Minnesela in 1881, placing it near the Redwater River, three miles southeast of the S & B Ranch. Here the promoters planned to sell lots, run businesses, including a flour mill and general store, and attract more farmers to the area. To ensure success, however, they hoped to convince the territorial legislature to carve a new county out of the existing Lawrence County, with their town as the county seat. When Lawrence County voters elected Bowman to the legislature in 1882, he successfully created Butte County, with Minnesela as the seat of government. Bowman, Chouteau, and Harrison were creating what they billed as "The Future Metropolis of the Black Hills."[17]

As Minnesela grew, Bullock established a love/hate relationship with the fledgling community and the outlying homesteaders. On the one hand, he saw the recent arrivals as a threat. He wanted the range south of his ranch left open for his animals, but the "sodbusters," as his men reportedly called them, interfered. He also hoped to establish his own town on the northern plains, but Minnesela temporarily preempted that plan. On the other hand, Bullock profited by selling equipment from his Deadwood and Spearfish stores to the new farmers. Then, too, when problems arose on the S & B Ranch, his employees could count on the residents of Minnesela for help. For instance, after a flood inundated the S & B Ranch, including the ranch house, in 1882, Harrison and others from Minnesela assisted in saving the livestock and the manager's family.[18]

With pressure from expanding cattle herds to the north and settlers to the southeast, Bullock decided to acquire more land. He had employees and associates, including Dominic Perrolio, either buy or claim land using federal land laws, such as the Homestead Act. Once these men gained title, sometimes by swearing false warrants, they sold their holdings to Bullock. This practice often violated the intent and the letter of the law, but Bullock and other ranchers paid no mind. Along with the property, Bullock acquired the adjoining water rights, allowing him to irrigate some of his pastures.[19] By the end of 1886, the S & B Ranch had expanded to 1,600 acres of what the newspaper called "choice land" at the intersection of the Redwater and Belle Fourche rivers.[20]

Situated between cattle ranches and homesteads, the S & B Ranch stood out as a unique enterprise. Bullock did not just raise cattle or concentrate on a single cash crop; instead, he put his land to a number of uses. He raised a variety of standard commodities, such as corn, oats, wheat, and cattle, but he also experimented with products new to the Black Hills. For example, as the open range disappeared and forage became limited, Bullock introduced alfalfa, which he had first seen growing in the Bear River Valley in Utah. Bullock had the agent of the Union Pacific Railroad send him the seed from Salt Lake City, and he planted it on his ranch in the spring of 1881. As others noticed the feed crop and its ability to sustain Bullock's animals, they readily adopted it. For years after, area farmers praised Bullock for this innovation.[21]

Not all of Bullock's experiments ended with such success. In another instance, he acquired Alderney cows. These animals are smaller than Guernsey cows, produce a richer milk, and were once popular with the landed gentry in England. While Bullock liked what they did and what they represented, the cows did not catch on, and Bullock sold his herd in 1886. When it came to agricultural ventures, Bullock again saw himself as a leader, willing to try new things. But his experiments did not always succeed, and seldom did they bring him much financial reward.[22]

Of all his ranch activities, Bullock spent the most time and money on breeding and selling horses. While horses were the backbone of everyday life and could be readily sold, Bullock did not handle average workhorses. Instead, he raised thoroughbred animals known as standardbred or, more commonly in Bullock's day, as Hambletonian horses.[23] Although these animals could be ridden, they were famous for their harness-racing abilities. Why Bullock selected this breed is unknown. Perhaps these fine racing animals appealed to his taste for the better things in life. Or, it may have been by chance. When the federal government stationed the Seventh Cavalry at Fort Meade in the late 1870s, Captain Frederick Benteen arrived with a Hambletonian stallion named Williamsburg. The *Black Hills Daily Times* raved about the animal, proclaiming Williamsburg "one of the finest appearing and decidedly the best bred horse in this country."[24] As Benteen anticipated leaving the area in 1881, Bullock and Star negotiated to buy the horse for their "fancy stock farm," and the paper supported their effort. "For the benefit of the country, in an equine point of view, it is hoped that they may succeed in getting him, and thus prevent his departure from the Hills country," the editor wrote.[25] The partners paid a thousand dollars for the stallion, and with this purchase, the newspaper noted, "The gentlemen believe in improving the stock in this country."[26]

After buying Williamsburg, Bullock took steps to ensure the success of his horse venture. Within three months of the purchase, he and Star imported several thoroughbred mares, again moving the newspaper to proclaim that in "four or five years they will have as fine a stable of blooded stock as can be found in any country."[27] In September of 1881, Bullock showed off Williamsburg at the Deadwood fair, but it took some time for his investments to bring returns.[28] His first sale of two-year old thoroughbreds sired by Williamsburg came in 1884, and this event caused the paper to declare that these animals "will make Dakota in the years to come as celebrated as the blue grass regions of Kentucky."[29] The next year, Bullock started racing his horses at Spearfish and at the Deadwood Driving Park, a racetrack located two miles east of town on the Boulder Canyon Road.[30]

Although Bullock had established a multifaceted ranch, he continually sought new ways to expand, and in 1884, a convergence of enterprises promised to bring more development and greater profits. Eighteen miles west of the S & B Ranch sat the Hay Creek coalfield. Since 1879, people in Deadwood had talked of building a railroad to the coal deposit, but little had happened except for some preliminary survey work in 1880. In 1884, Bullock reinvigorated the project, envisioning a rail line across his property, with a station located on his land. He called it the Deadwood & Redwater Railroad, and for the next two years, he invested, promoted, and tried to convince anyone who would listen of the virtues of the Hay Creek coal bank and his railroad.[31]

Bullock's enthusiasm for these projects stemmed, in part, from the possibilities they presented for a larger scheme. In 1884, the Northern Pacific Railroad had initiated discussions with local freighters about using Dickinson or the recently created town of Medora in northern Dakota as the transfer station for Black Hills-bound freight. Since 1876, freight from the Northern Pacific had arrived in Deadwood along the Bismarck Trail. A change in shipping points would mean a new route and lower rates for Deadwood merchants. Bullock wanted the line to run from Medora to Deadwood, with a stop on the S & B Ranch. To expedite this trail, he spearheaded the building of a bridge across the Belle Fourche River near the proposed station. If the road proved a success, Bullock anticipated that the Northern Pacific would next build a line down the trail from Medora, ultimately connecting with his Deadwood & Redwater Railroad and the Hay Creek coal beds.[32]

Bullock's work seemed to pay off when the Marquis deMores immediately started using the new bridge for his Black Hills Stage and Forwarding Company. DeMores, the son of a French nobleman, had become enamored with the western cattle industry like many Europeans in the early 1880s, but he thought he had a better idea. He planned to slaughter cattle in the northern range country and then use refrigerated cars to ship the meat east. In 1883, in the badlands of northwestern Dakota Territory, he established the town of Medora, naming it after his wife, and he built his headquarters and packing plant there. The next year, he decided to expand his empire by running stages and freight wagons to Deadwood, using Bullock's bridge as part of the route. The freight traffic started in the spring of 1884, and the stage operation began in October, with three coaches scheduled to leave Medora and Deadwood every week. The route had seven stage stops, including one on the S & B Ranch called DeMores.[33]

To Bullock, the birth of DeMores portended great things. While it started with only a saloon, cookhouse, dance hall, a Star and Bullock Hardware Store, and a few shacks, Bullock envisioned an urban center growing around two connecting rail lines. The editor of the Black Hills Daily Times proclaimed that it would be "in all probability the Denver of the Hills."[34] But after the first flurry of excitement, little else happened. By May 1885, the Marquis deMores announced that he was "sick and tired of the stage and forwarding business," and he wanted to sell.[35] The arrival of the Fremont, Elkhorn & Missouri Valley Railroad into the Black Hills in 1885 quickly terminated the nobleman's experiment. From its station at Buffalo Gap in the southern Hills, the Elkhorn captured the region's mail, freight, and passenger traffic, ending deMores's hope of a Black Hills empire and any chance of the Northern Pacific Railroad building south.[36]

The failure of the Medora trail temporarily halted Bullock's dream of a new urban center. The town of DeMores hung on for a time, with the saloon surviving on the local cowboy trade, but it too closed. The coal mines and the Redwater railroad went undeveloped. Beyond these disappointments, drought came to the grasslands in 1886, challenging the survival of the S & B Ranch itself. Thirsty cattle drifted into the river bottoms, eating the forage and wrecking crops.

These conditions forced Bullock and Star to buy extra feed for their animals, putting a drain on their capital.[37]

Despite the turn in fortunes, Bullock seemingly remained unconcerned. In part, his natural self-confidence allowed him to remain cool during difficult times, sure that things would work out for the better. Bullock also managed to ignore many day-to-day problems because he seldom ran his own businesses. For instance, Fred Fuller operated the ranch, while Bullock continued to live in Deadwood, visiting the spread only when necessary. Further, Bullock usually shared the financial risk with other business associates. Star, of course, partnered with him at the ranch, but others, like Alvin Fox, invested with him in the railroad venture. These arrangements allowed Bullock to move ahead with projects that would have scared away more cautious men.[38]

Even as Bullock expanded his ranch and hardware businesses, his attention remained focused on Deadwood. He realized that if Deadwood failed to recover after the fire of 1879 his efforts would mean little. For the town to thrive, businessmen needed to join together to transform it. Merchants, who had previously made Deadwood the commercial center of the northern Black Hills, had to reestablish their primacy and attract mining families to their rebuilt stores. Many potential customers lived in Central City and Lead City, not far away, but all roads to Deadwood were toll roads, and only a handful of people had transportation. Some store owners talked of building free roads; others dreamt of railroads.

A few promoters also sought to diversify the economy. In particular, they knew that several nearby mining districts sat quiet. Claims there had shown some values, but they contained "refractory" ore, which was different from the "free-milling" gold ore mined on the Homestake belt in Lead. Homestake miners used a simple mechanical process to remove the gold from their ore, while refractory ore required a more difficult chemical process. Businessmen in Deadwood talked about finding a way to treat the refractory ore, building a processing plant in their town, and then prospering from the new mining activity.[39]

As Bullock and a few others surveyed these challenges, they began advocating for a board of trade, something like a modern economic-development committee. Among this group, Bullock was the loudest and most persistent. After nearly a year of talking, a majority of businessmen agreed, and over fifty of them met in the Phoenix building in January 1881, one month before the city was incorporated. Here they created the Deadwood Board of Trade and established its objectives: "to encourage enterprise, that capital from abroad may come here for investment, to assist in building up and developing our resources."[40] They next chose a committee of seven, which included Bullock, to draft by-laws. The Black Hills Daily Times applauded the proceedings, reminding readers that "a board of trade for Deadwood has been Seth Bullock's pet hobby, and now that we have one, we suppose he is happy."[41]

Over the next year, the board of trade met several times to discuss potential projects, with each member promoting his own special interest. Bullock and fellow merchants James K. P. Miller and Harris Franklin, however, set the direction. They initially settled upon some small undertakings, such as sponsoring a Fourth of July celebration and publishing a promotional booklet entitled The Black Hills of Dakota, 1881. This publication's goal was to convince potential investors of Deadwood's "natural advantages."[42] The board then took on four larger projects: building a free road to Spearfish, constructing a flour mill, getting a railroad into Deadwood, and opening a smelter. In each case, Bullock played a role, serving on at least seven board of trade committees.[43]

During the board's initial meeting, Bullock stated "that the first thing they should turn their attention to are the highways leading into town," the *Times* recorded. "They were all toll roads, and these should be supplanted with free wagon roads." In particular, he wanted a road up City Creek to False Bottom Creek and then on to Spearfish. He said that it would shorten the trip by at least four miles and that the construction could be done in sixty days. He also indicated that the county commission might provide some financial backing.[44] Bullock, however, did not point out the obvious: he had the most to gain from the project. This route would provide him with better access to his property on upper False Bottom Creek and then to his ranch beyond. Nevertheless, the board agreed with him. Over the next several months, Bullock and the road committee sought "subscribers" (financial backers) in the local business community and among settlers on the plains, but they gained little support. Few were convinced of the undertaking's practicality. The board contracted for some preliminary grading, but it would take years before the route was finished.[45]

Not long after the Deadwood Board of Trade accepted Bullock's road proposal, it voted to support the construction of a flour mill. In a town so closely associated with gold mining, it seems odd that the board of trade's first industrial project would be a flour mill. But this development also happened, in part, because of Bullock's prodding and his belief in agriculture. When the mill proposal passed, he immediately offered another resolution. This one stated that Scotch Fife was the "most profitable wheat for both the producer and consumer" and that the "board of trade recommend and request the farmers of the Black Hills to procure and sow" that variety.[46] This motion similarly passed. The board as a whole hoped that the flour mill would serve as the nucleus for industrial development. They anticipated that it would inspire investors to open other factories in town, and, in their wildest dreams, they envisioned Deadwood "becoming to the [Black] Hills what Denver is to Colorado."[47]

The board of trade wanted a private developer to build the flour mill, with the board providing a five-thousand-dollar cash bonus upon its completion. To receive the money, the potential mill owner had to agree to a number of stipulations, including buying new equipment, spending more than twenty-five thousand dollars on the machinery, and building the mill within one-half mile of the Deadwood post office. While many people expressed interest, the board found no takers. All saw the requirements as too restrictive. The board amended the terms, and Robert Hood agreed to build the mill on upper Main Street.[48]

Hood finished the plant in December, and after examining the new four-story building and its three "roller machines," the newspaper exclaimed, "The time is near at hand when no more of the base of the staff of life will be imported."[49] At each step of the mill's development, Bullock played a part. He sat on the committee that crafted the board's guidelines, he helped raise the five thousand dollars, and when it looked like Hood would run out of money, he, Star, and Franklin invested in the project. While Hood managed the mill, these three men supported him as silent partners.[50]

Hood operated the mill over the next two years, producing "Board of Trade" and "S.S.S." brands of flour. He ran it only intermittently, however, and found the going tough. Bringing grain through the mountains added to the flour's cost, and flour mills in Spearfish and Minnesela provided stiff competition. Perhaps capitalizing on Bullock's connections as a deputy United States marshal, the mill gained government contracts to provide flour to several Sioux agencies, and these agreements helped the mill survive. Nevertheless, by mid-1884, Hood wanted out. In June, he sold his remaining share of the business to Bullock, Star, and Franklin. They reorganized the venture, naming Franklin president and Star secretary and general manager. Star would run the mill for the next twelve years, only surrendering the job when the plant burned in 1896. During this long span, Bullock played no apparent role in the flour mill's operation.[51]

Beyond free roads and a flour mill, the Deadwood Board of Trade knew that permanent prosperity would only come with rail connections, and in the first months of the board's operation, the members wondered how to attract a railroad. It would take some work, for in early 1881, the nearest rail lines were hundreds of miles away, with those in eastern Dakota Territory blocked by the Great Sioux Reservation. The problems outweighed the possibilities, until July, when word spread that the Homestake Mining Company was constructing its own railroad, the Black Hills & Fort Pierre. Homestake intended this line to be a logging railroad, but James K. P. Miller urged the board to visit with mine superintendent Samuel McMaster to see if he would extend it from Lead to Deadwood and then on to other mining camps. While the railroad would not have any outside connections, it would still revolutionize travel within the northern Black Hills, easily transporting people to Deadwood merchants. It sounded reasonable to Miller and the board, but in the end, McMaster and his board were not interested in Deadwood's problems. The Black Hills & Fort Pierre Railroad extended southwest out of Lead, in the opposite direction from Deadwood, as if intentionally ignoring its neighboring community.[52]

Bullock played no obvious part in the discussions with the Homestake, but he wanted railroads as badly as anyone. He showed this desire when word spread that the Wyoming Territorial Legislature and the Laramie County government in Cheyenne were going to help the Union Pacific extend its line from Cheyenne to Fort Laramie in early 1882. People in Deadwood became excited, believing this expansion was the first step in building to the Black Hills. After it had been inactive for a few months, the Deadwood Board of Trade rapidly convened to determine what they could do to make it happen. The board formed a committee of fifteen, which included Bullock and Miller, to undertake a railroad survey to determine what railroads might build to the Black Hills, how much money could be found in Lawrence County for construction, and if Pennington and Custer counties might provide some support. Bullock had the specific job of checking with the Chicago & North Western Railway to see if it intended to expand to the Black Hills. After more meetings and a banquet, where board of trade members heartily praised one another, the railroad discussions died again. Failure resulted from a lack of money and from the fact that the Union Pacific's extension to Fort Laramie never materialized. Deadwood boosters, however, remained on the alert for any and all railroad opportunities.[53]

Over the course of the railroad discussions, the Deadwood Board of Trade also considered a fourth project during the hectic year of 1881: the construction of a smelter. Just as the name sounds, a smelter exposes ore to intense heat, trying to melt the gold and silver out of the rock. This process had been used in Colorado since the late 1860s, and some in Deadwood saw it as a way to treat the area's refractory ores. The push to build a smelter took on new importance when prospectors uncovered silver ore some five miles northwest of Deadwood at a location known as Carbonate in 1881. In the view of Bullock, Miller, and Franklin, a smelter built in Deadwood would bring economic prosperity to their town, develop the new silver district, and awaken the refractory gold regions.[54]

Bullock and his associates, working through the board of trade, soon organized the Deadwood Smelting and Reduction Works. Their first problem was determining how to finance it. They created a stock company, offering twenty-five thousand shares of stock valued at one dollar each. They next asked for subscriptions, and board members promised to invest. Star and Bullock decided to take two thousand shares, as did Franklin, while Miller opted for one thousand. As other board of trade members bought stock, they selected Bullock, Franklin, and Miller as directors of the company. Their mission was the "erection and construction of a smelter and other desirable reduction works, the purchase and reduction of ores and the acquisition of mines and working of the same."[55] But by the spring of 1882, miners at Carbonate had found little silver ore, and the talk of a smelter quieted down. The idea had nevertheless been planted, and many continued to think that a smelter could help the neighboring mining districts and bring a new industrial base to town.[56]

Of the four major projects that Bullock and the Deadwood Board of Trade worked on in 1881, only the flour mill became a reality. The others failed, in part, because the board met inconsistently. If a project suddenly seemed important, the members quickly called a meeting and debated their options. In between these moments of activity, the board got together only sporadically, and projects often died for lack of attention. In December 1882, for example, the Times sarcastically reported that a package addressed to the board was at the post office "awaiting to be called for. For all that we know to the contrary, the package will remain in its present quarters and eventually become a fixture of the place."[57] Bullock's interest rose and fell just as rapidly as the board's, causing him to provide inconsistent leadership. Bullock enjoyed coming up with big ideas, but he generally expected someone else to follow through on the concept. It must be mentioned, however, that throughout this period Bullock had the stores and ranch to distract him from the board's activities.

A crisis developed in 1883 that caused members of the Deadwood Board of Trade to meet again, but not for the sake of economic development. In the spring of that year, Whitewood Creek began to rise, causing many to take precautions against flooding. Bullock, for example, had men form a levee around his building with bags of ground oats. Barriers, however, could not stop the water that roared down the gulch in May. The flood pulled some buildings apart and inundated others. The newspaper estimated the immediate loss at almost two hundred thousand dollars, with Bullock and Star suffering ten thousand dollars in damages. In response, a few community leaders, including Bullock and Miller, formed another "citizens' committee" to inspect Whitewood Creek's channel and recommend ways to prevent another flood.[58]

When the committee delivered its findings, it offered two recommendations. The first was for an unobstructed creek channel of at least fifty feet in width. Prior to the flood, property owners had deflected the creek to suit their needs, often building in and over the channel. Bullock and Miller's committee then recommended building a bulkhead along the course of the creek. Made of log cribbing, sixteen feet high and twelve feet wide at the base, this dirt-filled structure would run for 1,060 feet on the west side of Whitewood Creek, thereby protecting the buildings on Main Street. The city commissioners agreed to these measures, but they lacked the money for construction. So, once again, Miller and others went from business to business taking subscriptions. The memory of the recent flood brought a strong response, and the contractor finished the project in October 1883. This first bulkhead started the process of confining Whitewood Creek to a defined channel, many feet below street level, which Deadwood would continue doing over the next several years.[59]

In buoyant frontier towns, disasters brought action, and in Deadwood, Bullock, Miller, and other businessmen worked to make sure their town survived and thrived, no matter the setback. While the 1883 flood required some rebuilding, the 1879 fire had necessitated a complete reconstruction. For many, these disasters forced a reexamination of their goals and ambitions, with some people moving away. Bullock, however, refused to be defeated. He used his experience in retail and agriculture to build again. But not only was he expanding his stores and ranch in the early 1880s and promoting Deadwood, he was also venturing into the unfamiliar territories of banking and mining in order to bring more prosperity to his community and greater profits to himself.

5

A Frenzy of Speculation

Much of what Bullock did after the fire of 1879 was about regeneration and redevelopment, giving Deadwood and his businesses new life. Yet, he also realized that new opportunities existed, especially if Deadwood regained its affluence. Consequently, as Bullock expanded his farm and his stores, he simultaneously went into banking and mining, obvious activities for a Deadwood businessman but previously untried by him. As Bullock put his career as a politician and sheriff further behind him in the early 1880s, he delved more and more into speculative ventures.

Bullock recognized that growth only came with plenty of capital. He promoted the Deadwood Board of Trade with the idea of attracting more outside money into town, but he also took a position with a bank that could provide additional local resources. In early 1880, pioneer banker William R. Stebbins reorganized his Deadwood holdings into a new firm called Merchants' National Bank. He issued 1,000 shares of stock, keeping 605 for himself and selling the remainder in small lots. Bullock acquired 25 shares, and Alvin Fox, the bank's cashier and general manager, purchased 50. Despite Bullock's relatively small investment, Stebbins named him bank president, probably based on the former sheriff's reputation and on the significant amount of business he had done with the bank. Even though Bullock had the highest office, Alvin Fox actually ran the enterprise, with Stebbins making many of the important decisions. Bullock primarily provided oversight, but he certainly influenced loans and investment decisions.[1]

With only two national banks in Deadwood, the Merchants' bank attracted a number of customers during its first years. But when banker R. E. Driscoll discussed the Merchants' activities some years later, he noted that Stebbins had done business "on somewhat of a 'shoestring' and was on rather thin ice."[2] Indeed, Stebbins and Fox took some chances. Most significantly, the bank invested in development of the Carbonate Mining District when it opened in 1881. Carbonate, however, did not immediately prosper, and as its fortunes rose and fell over the next five years, so did the condition of the Merchants' bank. By 1886, word spread that the bank was overextended, and its depositors lost confidence. When the Deadwood National Bank opened in the fall of 1886, customers began moving their accounts, and finally on 17 February 1887, the Merchants' bank failed to open its doors.[3]

The bank's failure stunned Deadwood. Mayor Sol Star worried about violence as the bank's creditors surrounded the building, demanding payment. To preserve peace, he ordered all gambling halls, saloons, and "similar resorts" closed for the day.[4] Cashier Alvin Fox tried to reassure the community by saying that he closed the bank as a precaution after an unexplained run threatened to deplete the bank's reserves. How Bullock responded to these events has not been recorded. Certainly, the action threatened what he had deposited in the bank, and it must have sent a shudder through his businesses. In fact, Bullock may have seen the trouble coming. Shortly before the closure, he unsuccessfully tried to remove himself from the board. Luckily for Bullock and his reputation, however, the community did not blame him for the closing.[5]

Two months after Fox closed the doors, Stebbins reopened the bank. Working with a federal bank examiner, he had developed a reorganization strategy. The plan required that Stebbins contribute more capital to the bank and that other stockholders, including Bullock, contribute more assets. Also, other major depositors needed to guarantee that they would not immediately remove their money. As he got these assurances, Stebbins apparently blamed Fox for the bank's poor performance and removed him as cashier. When the bank reopened, Bullock did his part. He held fast and continued to serve on the board of directors, at least for a time, although he no longer held the title of president. The reorganized Merchants' National Bank operated until the First National Bank absorbed it in 1894.[6]

Just as the Merchants' bank saw opportunities in the Carbonate Mining District, so did Bullock himself. In fact, he probably encouraged some of the bank's investments. Yet, he entered the mining industry with little experience. He owned just two hardrock claims in the Bald Mountain Mining District and some placer ground near Deadwood. None of these locations produced any gold or silver. Bullock, however, paid close attention to prospector James Redpath's stories of discovering carbonate ore, a silver-lead combination, five miles northwest of Deadwood in 1881. After touring the new Carbonate Mining District, Bullock joined with other investors to organize two mining companies, the Eureka and the Iron Hill, setting up stock-based corporations. The latter company looked the most promising because it controlled six claims, including some of the first found in the district, such as the Utica. The vein of ore at this location was at least one foot wide, with obvious mineralization. When he put samples on display in the window of the Merchants' National Bank, the glint in the ore spread a buzz throughout town. People immediately began clamoring for stock. As a founding member, Bullock acquired a number of shares in the company and facilitated the sale of more. Yet, he initially took no role in management, not even serving on the board of directors; his other enterprises were most likely occupying his time.[7]

As people studied the Carbonate ore samples, they speculated that mining activity there would bring another boom. The Deadwood Board of Trade talked about building a smelter to capitalize on the new ore, hoping to foster another success such as the Homestake. As the mines on the Homestake belt yielded more and more wealth, they brought prosperity to Lead City and Central City. Deadwood businessmen hoped the Carbonate district would do the same for their town. They also recognized that men in California, led by George Hearst, owned and benefited most from the Homestake mine. Those who invested locally in the Carbonate mines hoped to become home-grown bonanza kings, and the names Carbonate and Iron Hill reflected their ambitions. Both labels were borrowed from locations near Leadville, Colorado, where the discovery of silver-lead ore in 1878 made millionaires of such local investors as Horace Tabor.

Success, however, did not follow. The first Carbonate mines, including the Iron Hill Company, operated intermittently and produced little profitable ore. In 1883, Iron Hill stockholders decided to make a change, and they put Seth Bullock, Alvin Fox, and D. A. McPherson, cashier of the First National Bank, on the board to capitalize on the men's financial leverage and business acumen. Under their direction, the Iron Hill Company became more active. Its fourteen employees pushed the shaft deeper and explored for more ore. In the process, they encountered small bodies of high-grade material, but not enough to sustain full-scale operations or even to pay for the ongoing work. The lack of revenue forced the board to levy an assessment against its stock, a method mining companies often used to raise funds. The board ordered a one-cent assessment to cover the cost of the shaft, meaning that each stockholder had to submit a penny for each share owned. The company had 250,000 shares on the market, and the assessment raised $2,500.

If a shareholder did not pay, the board listed the stock as delinquent and sold it again. Bullock reportedly held 22,000 shares of stock, costing him $220 on a one-cent assessment. Considering that Iron Hill shares had cost just pennies to begin with, assessments significantly drove up the owners' investments and their need for future profits.[8]

Exploration and development continued through 1884 and into 1885, with the miners uncovering more ore. Some of it was free milling, and the silver could be easily liberated through crushing and amalgamation. Other samples, however, indicated refractory ore, requiring smelting to free the metal. Because the Iron Hill Company had neither a crushing mill nor a smelter, it had to rely on other firms to treat all its ore. Fortunately, Nathan Hattenbach opened a small smelter one mile from the Iron Hill mine in October 1884, and the Iron Hill directors contracted with him to process their ore. When Hattenbach fired up his smelter, a mixture of silver and lead began pouring out of the furnace, and six weeks later, the Iron Hill Company made its first shipment. People from Carbonate Camp to Deadwood broke into celebration as forty-two silver-lead bullion bars, weighing around one hundred pounds apiece, arrived at the Merchants' National Bank and went on display in the bank's window.[9] With the newspaper estimating the bullion's value at $1 per ounce, the bars represented $67,200, and Iron Hill stock, which had been selling for three cents a share, quickly jumped to over a dollar. Other mining company stocks soared as well, and the press quickly hailed Carbonate Camp as a "second Leadville."[10]

The relationship between the Hattenbach smelter and the Iron Hill Company soon broke down, however, leaving Bullock and the other directors uncertain about what to do next. The company's superintendent decided to put some high-grade ore in bags and ship it to a smelter in Omaha, a costly but necessary alternative. For the venture to be profitable, board members reasoned that they needed to expand the mine and build their own processing plant. As they discussed options, they changed leadership again, this time making Seth Bullock president. The choice seems surprising. His mining experience was limited to buying and selling claims, and he had no background in underground mining or in the operation of mills or smelters. Perhaps the board chose him for his public persona. People trusted him, and if things did not go well, he could deflect stockholders' criticisms. Or maybe Bullock himself wanted to assume more leadership responsibilities, hoping to make the mine a success. No matter the reason, for the next five years he would lead the Iron Hill Company. In practical terms, by the mid-1880s Bullock was simultaneously heading up at least four different ventures: the Star & Bullock hardware stores, the S & B Stock Farm, the Merchants' National Bank, and the Iron Hill mining company.[11]

As Bullock took charge, the Iron Hill board publicly announced the purchase of a new hoisting works and a complete mill. The directors made the acquisitions known because the projects required more assessments. With silver bullion coming from Iron Hill, stockholders were expecting dividends and not more expenses. The board recognized their concern and made the announcement to deflect anxiety and prevent the stock from dropping. Throughout Bullock's career as president, he and the board worked hard to keep the stock prices as high as possible. Low prices decreased the worth of their own investments, threatened their positions on the board, and limited their opportunities to sell stock in the other mines they controlled. Despite the warning, when the assessments came, the stock fell.[12]

With money from the assessments, the board decided to build a ten-stamp mill with amalgamation tables, a standard configuration for treating free-milling silver ore. The board members chose this type of mill over a smelter because they believed that the mine contained vast quantities of free-milling ore. They, however, continued to send the high-grade refractory material to the Omaha smelter. By the time the Iron Hill mill started operating in November 1885, the board had raised $82,500 through multiple assessments. This amount meant that each stockholder had contributed thirty-three cents per share, with Bullock responsible for $7,260, a significant investment in the future of the mine.[13]

The new mill did not disappoint. The superintendent claimed that it saved ninety percent of the silver, and by December, it was reportedly producing between a thousand and fifteen hundred dollars in bullion everyday. As the bars collected in the mine office, one of the directors, oftentimes Bullock, would bring five or six to Deadwood, stacking them in the window of the Merchants' bank. With each bar weighing over a thousand ounces, and each ounce estimated to be worth a little over a dollar, the public gawked at the thousands of dollars of silver-lead bullion on display.[14]

As the storied Treasure Coach left town loaded with Black Hills silver, many thought a new day was dawning, and when the Iron Hill directors declared their first dividend, all were convinced it had arrived. The initial dividend of a nickel per share went out in early February 1886, and others followed at monthly intervals until August. The six dividends distributed $75,000, a welcome reward to the long-suffering stockholders. Yet, that amount fell short of what investors had paid through assessments. Nevertheless, the payments brought hope, and as the Black Hills Daily Times commented after one dividend, "Many a Deadwoodite will be $50 or $100 better off at the close of the day."[15] The stock's price soared. Where the shares had a value of a few cents each by late 1885, in early May 1886 the price had advanced to $7.50 a share.[16]

As the stock shot up, a flourishing exchange developed in Deadwood. With no organized market, buyers, sellers, and brokers gathered in front of Merchants' National Bank and

First National Bank to do their trading. These two banks sat on the west side of Main Street, with only a narrow section of Lee Street separating them. Locals called it the Bank Corner. The *Times* described this impromptu gathering site as a "monster exchange."[17] Here, shares rapidly changed hands, with some transactions totaling over a hundred thousand dollars. Most sales, however, were much smaller, but during the Iron Hill boom, many Deadwood people invested and prospered.[18] One observer pointed out that everyone who lived on Williams Street, a prestigious section of town, owned stock in the mine, and the area soon became known as Iron Hill Row.[19]

The *Black Hills Daily Times* took great joy in the proceedings. At the peak of the excitement in April 1886, it proclaimed, "Main street during the palmiest days of '77, or at any subsequent date no matter what the attraction, was scarcely more crowded, and excitement never ran higher, than on yesterday."[20] The paper also reveled in the fact that Deadwood residents held most of the stock, claiming it brought "great benefit to the city."[21] Indeed, the Iron Hill's apparent success brought changes. Developers began constructing buildings, and the *Times* reported, "Another month's work will so completely transmogrify the metropolis that absentees upon returning will scarcely recognize the city."[22] From the newspaper's perspective, another Leadville or Comstock Lode was at hand, "only on a grander scale."[23] And the reporter gave Seth Bullock and the other directors credit, stating that they had "inspired confidence, stimulated work and indirectly accomplished great developments throughout the entire Hills."[24]

Not only did the Iron Hill boom transform Deadwood, but it also brought a new mineral rush. Speculators, investors, and promoters dashed to the Black Hills in 1886 to buy stock in what they hoped was the next great bonanza. The Ruby Basin and Bald Mountain mining districts to the southwest of Deadwood gained attention, as did the Galena area directly to the south, but most money men focused on Carbonate Camp. New companies formed, such as the Silver Hill, Silver Ridge, Segregated Iron Hill, Endymion, Tail of the Comet, and Ruby Bell, just to name a few. Over forty new companies offered stock in May of 1886, with the public rapidly snapping up the shares. By June, one hundred and sixty-four incorporated mining companies existed in the northern Black Hills, with seventy of those in the Carbonate district. The Iron Hill directors, including Bullock, played a key role in creating and developing several of these ventures, buying stock in each. While the shares only cost a few pennies, hundreds of purchases added up to substantial sums of money. Then, because of his success at the Iron Hill Company, thirteen of the new operations named Bullock president. And most of these nascent mines immediately started levying assessments.[25]

While the mining excitement gripped Deadwood, the Fremont, Elkhorn & Missouri Valley Railroad began building toward Rapid City. With the Elkhorn so close, an outside rail connection seemed likely, something that James K. P. Miller and a few others deemed absolutely necessary for permanent prosperity. Bullock more practically recognized that a rail line would reduce transportation costs for his businesses, especially for the Iron Hill operation with its heavy shipments. But to make sure it happened, Miller, Bullock, and other board of trade members gathered for their first formal meeting in two years. Following Miller's advice, the board sent a committee east, with Miller at the head, to confer with the Elkhorn officers. The railroad president gave the men some vague assurances about building to Deadwood, and all seemed satisfied as they headed home. In July 1886, Bullock, Miller, Sol Star, and a few other Deadwood notables traveled to Rapid City to welcome the first passenger train. While celebrating, the Deadwood men cornered visiting railroad officials and re-emphasized their desire for an immediate extension, but despite assurances, these efforts brought little. The Elkhorn stopped building once it reached Rapid City.[26]

While Bullock supported the railroad, he also had other priorities. When the reinvigorated Deadwood Board of Trade met, he brought up the free road to Spearfish, which had been started in 1881 but never completed. He wanted it finished, with an extension to Carbonate Camp. Even though Bullock and his Iron Hill mine would naturally benefit, many in Deadwood also considered the road a necessity during the Carbonate boom.[27] To get the board's support, Bullock took Miller, who had become the moving force behind the board of trade, to Carbonate Camp to convince him of the need. Miller came back in full agreement, stating that he could not understand why "the road was not constructed long ago."[28] To this end, the board began raising funds, and crews went to work, but again money ran low, and the grading remained unfinished.[29]

Beyond Bullock's concern for roads and railroads, he knew that the Iron Hill boom of early 1886 did not guarantee long-term success, especially since the Iron Hill mill had only ten stamps and could not treat the refractory ore. To expand and enhance the operation, he decided to add ten more stamps, doubling the mill's free-milling capacity, and to buy the Hattenbach smelter to treat the refractory ores locally. In the wake of the company's strong performance and ongoing dividends, the announcement of these improvements should have buoyed confidence and driven up stock prices. Instead, the value of shares fell from a previous high of $7.50 in early May 1886 to $1.50 in late July. Prices appeared to stabilize and even rebound over the next few months as the company blew in the smelter. Then in November, the stock collapsed again, falling to a low of fifty-five cents. As the Iron Hill Company went down, other mines followed, causing a general financial panic.[30]

In an interview with the *Black Hills Daily Times*, Bullock declared the collapse "senseless," and the editor agreed, seeing no rational reason for the downturn.[31] Yet, the newspaper published several possible explanations why stockholders had lost faith. One was the fact that the number of silver bullion bars arriving in Deadwood had gone down during the second half of 1886. The drop in production fed rumors already circulating that the ore body was exhausted or that the free-milling ore was gone, leaving only refractory material. The company had inadvertently added to this speculation when it purchased the Hattenbach smelter to treat the more difficult ore. The negative stories only increased as problems in constructing the new stamp mill and in running the smelter disrupted operations. Other hearsay suggested that banker Stebbins was manipulating the stock price. Some believed that Stebbins wanted a lower price so that he and his bank could buy more shares and profit when their value rebounded. Then in November, the rumors of a failed mine seemed verified when the superintendent resigned, claiming no more ore existed.[32]

As stock prices dropped and gossip spread, Bullock made every effort to explain away the concerns and return the company to public favor. He confidently stated to the newspapers that two hundred thousand dollars of ore sat on the dump, but he admitted that the silver content had decreased and that the ore had changed from free-milling to more refractory. The stamp mill could now only recover fifty-three percent of the metal, but Bullock remained convinced that the smelter could make up the difference. Unfortunately, the Hattenbach device had many problems, but they could be fixed. If the smelter could not be repaired, then the company would continue shipping ore to Omaha. As a testament to his faith in the mine, he invited Deadwood citizens to tour the facilities, and he bought five thousand additional shares of stock at $2.50 each. He hoped this action would stabilize the price and inspire other stockholders to do the same.[33] As he told the *Times* reporter on another occasion, "Tell the boys to stand pat."[34] His dedication got noticed. When his workers extended the mine into some new ore, they named it the "Bullock level."[35] His pronouncements, however, did not have any effect on the stock's price. It continued to slide to the low point of fifty-five cents a share. Then, in the ultimate statement of his perseverance and confidence, when the superintendent resigned, Bullock took on the job of general manager.[36]

By early 1887, the fortunes of the Iron Hill Company had seemingly turned. The stamp mill had closed permanently, but the refitted Hattenbach smelter was again producing base bullion. As bars began appearing in Deadwood, the company's stock advanced to over a dollar a share. Those still holding stock hoped that profit-takers had sold out and speculation had ended. They, like Bullock, wanted to make this mine a long-term proposition, and the newspaper report of 6 February 1887 embodied their hopes: "Iron Hill is not a mine for a day. Its permanency is established beyond peradventure or doubt."[37]

To guarantee continuous production, however, the company needed a better smelter—the Hattenbach being too small and too expensive to operate. Bullock pushed for a new, larger facility, but Alvin Fox resisted. Building a smelter meant voting against dividends, which would drive down the stock. Fox, cashier at Merchants' bank, wanted more dividends and higher stock prices. His bank had made a number of loans and investments based on the value of Iron Hill stock, and the crash in 1886 had seriously hurt its operation. For the sake of the bank's cash flow, Fox needed better financial returns. In the end, Fox resigned from the board in early February, and the remaining members voted to build the smelter. Two weeks later, the Merchants' National Bank failed.[38]

As the new Iron Hill plant went up next to the old one in Rubicon Gulch, other mine owners complained that it should have been placed in Bullock's hometown. They felt that Deadwood's more central location would have allowed mines in other districts, such as Ruby Basin, Bald Mountain, and Galena, to ship in ore more easily. Bullock's people responded that their mine would keep the smelter busy and that they did not want outside ore, but Bullock himself remained quiet. As a member of the board of trade, promoter of Deadwood, and one of the original organizers of the Deadwood Smelting and Reduction Works in 1881, Bullock should have been a supporter of the Deadwood site, but he apparently saw the practicality of building the plant closer to the mine. Harris Franklin, James K. P. Miller, and other businessmen, on the other hand, were determined to erect a treatment plant in Deadwood. After six years of watching local smelters fail, they decided to investigate processing techniques used in other mining camps, and from 1887 into 1888, the Deadwood investors explored treatment options.[39]

Meanwhile, the Iron Hill smelter began operating in June 1887. With its opening, the newspaper praised Bullock, stating that he "never for a moment faltered or wavered in his faith in the mine, and who more than any other single stockholder is to be credited with the erection of the new plant."[40] The price of Iron Hill stock reacted, hovering around two dollars a share, its highest point in eight months. Old stockholders and new investors anticipated great success. When 150 bullion bars showed up in Deadwood two days later, the paper exclaimed that it must be the first of "undoubtedly a continuous series of shipments."[41] And as more bars followed, the company became more vigorous. It sank new shafts, did exploratory work, and declared a dividend in September, the first in nearly a year.[42]

The renewal of dividends brought jubilation throughout the region. Confidence spread, and as Iron Hill stock continued to go up, the paper reflected on the Iron Hill operations. It argued that when the company purchased the Hattenbach smelter, it was a "forlorn hope," stating that the men who ran it "knew nothing practically of a smelter." The paper then commented that since the new smelter began running, "the debts have all been paid off," new discoveries have been made, and capitalists were again anxious to invest in Iron Hill stock. "President Bullock and the directors are entitled to the greatest praise for their management of the Iron Hill," the reporter concluded.[43]

By early November, and after two more dividends, the company's stock sold for nearly three dollars a share, but then another slide began. The *Black Hills Daily Times* found the dip completely mystifying, especially since it began as the board declared yet another dividend. Rumors of poor ore seemed to drive the sell-off, but the Iron Hill men remained positive, claiming that the outlook could not be brighter. When the company skipped December's dividends, the rumors seemed to be confirmed. For those who tried to maintain faith, disaster struck when the smelter closed at the end of February 1888, driving the stock down to twenty-five cents a share. Three months earlier, Bullock had said there was nothing discouraging in the mine, but he told a reporter in March that low-grade ore had forced the closing. He, however, remained hopeful, confident that good ore still existed. Then just days after the smelter shutdown, Bullock and the other board members compounded the gloom, declaring a seven-and-a-half-cent assessment in order to raise $18,750 to pay off operating costs.[44]

As the Iron Hill stock fell from November 1887 through March 1888, stockholders expressed their frustrations. The newspaper stated that "denunciations are heard on every hand," but it maintained that such should be expected since Iron Hill stock was locally owned.[45] The cries grew louder with the assessment, and the newspaper responded that condemnation of the board was "unreasonable and undeserved. . . . The directors may have made mistakes, but we believe they are honest."[46] If the stockholders wanted action, the editor opined, they could elect a new board. Yet, when the stockholders met for their annual meeting in June, they retained the old board, keeping Bullock as president, a job he would hold for another three years. Over that time, he struggled to bring the mine back to productivity.[47]

Bullock's challenges at the Iron Hill Company paralleled problems he was having elsewhere, and by 1887, disaster seemed to haunt his affairs. While the failure of the Merchants' National Bank undoubtedly hurt his finances, the collapse of the Iron Hill Company was devastating. Additional economic distress, however, came from his stock farm. Problems had started there with the drought of 1886, when the lack of grass forced Bullock to buy extra feed for his animals, diverting needed assets. Then, during the winter of 1886-1887, ice and snow covered the range. Many ranchers lost over seventy-five percent of their animals.[48] Bullock's losses were not recorded but can be surmised through his comments to the Deadwood newspaper. After a trip to his ranch, Bullock reported that his cows froze standing up, but with a warm wind, they thawed out and returned to grazing. He went on to speculate that he could freeze his stock every fall and "lay the carcasses away until spring." In preserving this rare sample of Bullock's humor, the Black Hills Daily Times called it Bullock's "theory of suspended animation."[49] Among the winter's casualties was Bullock and Star's prized horse. Williamsburg suffered a leg injury during the winter and died the following summer.[50]

The financial losses from farming, mining, and banking sent shock waves through Bullock's economic empire, especially because he had overextended himself to make the investments. His cash-flow problems seemed to have started in 1885 when the Lawrence County tax records show Bullock and Star delinquent on their property taxes. Court notices began appearing in the newspapers, indicating legal actions for the recovery of loans. These problems would continue over the next several years as their financial condition worsened. Unfortunately for Star, wherever Bullock's fortunes led, Star's followed. Even though Star had little interest in the Iron Hill project or the bank, the pair remained partners in the hardware stores and the farm. As Bullock took business chances, his successes or failures affected all his enterprises, including Star's investments.[51]

Bullock took a variety of actions to deflect his financial problems. To protect property from foreclosure, he transferred some to his wife's name. To remove personal liability from his main businesses, he and Star incorporated the Deadwood Star & Bullock Hardware Company and the S & B Stock Farm in 1886. In both cases, Fred Eccles joined Bullock and Star as one of the three incorporators. In a final move to ensure stability, Star and Bullock Hardware joined with another Deadwood hardware dealer in 1887, still operating under the Star and Bullock name.[52] The Black Hills Daily Times reported that the consolidation made the business "one of the strongest, financially" in the region.[53]

Bullock's attempt to secure the farm's operation began with incorporation, but he needed to generate revenue, as well. He sold his Alderney cows and became more aggressive in the horse business. In September 1887, the S & B Stock Farm held its first annual horse sale, coinciding with the Deadwood fair. Advertising the sale of two-, three-, and four-year-old colts suitable for harness racing, Bullock stated, "Any one of these colts can win this fall in his class the amount that he will sell for."[54] The next summer,

Bullock took the dramatic step of shipping twelve horses to a breeders' exposition in Chicago to sell as "blooded stock." For the trip, he decorated the railroad car with flags, streamers, and a large banner that proclaimed: "'Black Hills flyers . . . from S. and B. stock farm, Deadwood, Dakota.'"[55] Bullock also bought horses to strengthen his bloodlines, but not all purchases went well. A valuable stallion, imported from Kentucky, died one week after arriving in the West. Nevertheless, Bullock continued selling, buying, and racing horses into 1891.[56]

Even as Bullock consolidated and retuned his hardware and farm businesses, he continued to seek ways to help his mining investments. In 1887, Harris Franklin, by this time one of Deadwood's most successful businessmen, became a member of the Iron Hill board of directors. When Franklin organized the Golden Reward Mining Company, Bullock joined him on the board of that new enterprise. Then, as the Iron Hill smelter closed in early 1888, Bullock understandably became much more interested in the processing plant that Franklin and Miller had been promoting for lower Deadwood. Organizers had changed the name from the Deadwood Smelting and Reduction Works to the more accurate Deadwood Reduction Works and had hired R. D. Clark of Cortez, Nevada, to build it. Clark claimed to have a special process, known only to himself, that could effectively treat the area's refractory gold and silver ores. His assurances enthused the organization, and a subscription committee canvassed town, with Bullock promising a two-thousand-dollar contribution. Soon after, Bullock was elected to the board of directors, becoming a member of the executive committee. As Clark built the reduction works in late 1888, Franklin trusted it would successfully treat his Golden Reward ore, and Bullock desperately hoped it could handle the low-grade Iron Hill material that his smelter could not.[57]

Before the Deadwood Reduction Works could produce an ounce of gold or silver, it burned to the ground on 1 March 1889. The fire had a suspicious origin, most likely set by Clark to hide the failure of his process, but the calamity would not defeat Franklin. It only encouraged the business-man to build his own ore-treatment plant for the Golden Reward property. It also forced Bullock to look yet again for another process to treat his ore. This time he found Franklin Carpenter and pyritic smelting. In 1889, Carpenter, dean of the Dakota School of Mines at Rapid City, had been experimenting with his own version of the smelting process, one that would treat the area's refractory ores more effectively and inexpensively. As Carpenter perfected the process in his lab, Bullock and James K. P. Miller came to watch. After the failure of the Clark plant, Miller and Bullock had become disenchanted with chemical processes, looking once again at smelting. Bullock brought some Iron Hill samples to Carpenter's lab for a trial run in August 1889.[58] The first test proved unsatisfactory, but two subsequent trials recovered the precious metals successfully, leading Bullock to announce: "To the Iron Hill company belongs the credit of inaugurating the process of pyritic or dry smelting."[59]

While Bullock took credit for establishing the validity of the pyritic process, Miller made it work. In the fall of 1889, Miller and his group of investors, known as the Syndicate, built a small smelter in lower Deadwood, across Whitewood Creek from the site of the burned Deadwood Reduction Works. Known as the "baby smelter" because of its small, experimental size, it established Carpenter's new smelting technique as commercially viable. In the meantime, Bullock experimented with the pyritic process at his smelter in Rubicon Gulch, beginning in December 1889. Throughout the month, Bullock and his smelter-men tried different combinations of ores, fuels, and fluxes with little luck.[60] To the anxious newspaperman covering the operation, Bullock explained: "There are no written or printed rules that can be followed successfully in pyritic smelting." The reporter, however, commented that Bullock "thinks he is on the right track."[61] Bullock announced that he had the process figured out, but suddenly his smelter closed—for good. He explained that the lack of transportation facilities and consequent high price of coke prevented continuous operations. In reality, the original pyritic process did not work well. Miller and Carpenter would build a large, pyritic smelter in lower Deadwood, but they used extra material that Bullock did not know about. Without this knowledge, he had little chance for success.[62]

After Bullock's test of the pyritic process, the Iron Hill Company did little mining or smelting. Some exploration for ore continued, but the management insisted that high shipping costs limited what they could do. With failure apparent, Franklin resigned as a director, and the Iron Hill board meeting of June 1890 broke down into a fight between pro-Bullock and anti-Bullock factions. In the end, a compromise board was elected, with Bullock retaining the presidency. After another year of inactivity, Bullock chose not to run for reelection at the annual meeting in 1891. Some stockholders tried to convince him to retain his position, but he knew the mine was done.[63]

Bullock had taken a chance on mining, and he lost. This failure must have been a personal and financial blow. Up until the end, Bullock kept faith in the project. In mid-1890, he published an account of what the company had done, believing it indicated success. The report showed that the Iron Hill Company had produced nearly $725,000 in bullion from 1883 into 1890 and had paid over $156,000 in dividends, but it had also levied about $149,000 in assessments. Of these, Bullock's portion probably amounted to $13,860 in dividends and $13,200 in assessments. His profit of $660 seems insignificant when his disbursements and commitments are considered.[64] For instance, he seldom sold the stock for more than what he paid. In total, he probably lost thousands of dollars from his Iron Hill purchases and from his investments in neighboring mines. Also, he contributed a vast amount of time to the presidency, no doubt an unpaid position, and he often traveled for the company without the benefit of an expense account. He worked hard to make this mining venture succeed, as he did with all his businesses, but his speculative adventures only brought him problems during the second half of the 1880s. He, however, would persevere. Moneymaking opportunities still existed, and he remained poised to take advantage of them.

6 Recovery

As Bullock struggled with the Iron Hill Company and tried to strengthen his other businesses, he fell more deeply into financial difficulties. But relief appeared to be on the horizon. In 1887, the Fremont, Elkhorn & Missouri Valley Railroad started building north of Rapid City. Once again Deadwood boosters anticipated a rail connection. Instead, the Elkhorn built along the eastern edge of the Black Hills, stopping nine miles northeast of Deadwood at the new town of Whitewood. Established by the Pioneer Townsite Company, a subsidiary of the railroad, Whitewood would serve as the end of track for the next three years, and from there the railroad could monopolize the traffic to and from Deadwood, without having to build through the mountains. Similarly, the residents of Minnesela had anticipated the rail line building to their town, but with the construction of cattle pens at Whitewood, the railroad needed to go no farther.[1]

The Elkhorn's actions frustrated Deadwood and Minnesela boosters alike, and few knew how to respond. Deadwood's leading rail enthusiast, James K. P. Miller, however, began visiting with the officers of a competing line, the Burlington & Missouri River Railroad. They had built through Nebraska during the 1880s, and Miller wanted them to extend into the Black Hills and Deadwood, outflanking the Elkhorn. Miller also tried to make the region more attractive to the Burlington. In 1888, just after the Elkhorn's extension to Whitewood, he organized his own railway, the Deadwood Central, with the hope of generating some local prosperity. His line would extend in two directions. First, he would build an interurban link between Deadwood and Lead, opening the Deadwood market to a new clientele. Second, he envisioned an extension to the Bald Mountain and Ruby Basin mining districts. By hauling ore to his smelter and to Harris Franklin's Golden Reward plant, he anticipated reinvigorating the mines in those areas. Miller also reasoned that the Deadwood Central would stimulate enough business to encourage the Burlington to build into Deadwood, but he had one more inducement up his sleeve. He offered to share, for a price, his railroad's right-of-way and roadbed with the new arrival.[2]

Miller's work brought results. As the Burlington built south of the Black Hills, heading for the coal fields of Wyoming, it announced a branch line to Deadwood that would run through the center of the Black Hills, with a possible connection to the cattle country in Butte County. The Elkhorn saw the Burlington's move as a threat to its monopoly and made plans to build extensions from Whitewood to Deadwood and the rangelands north of the Hills. For area residents, their long frustrations appeared over as the Elkhorn began construction in 1890. In particular, Deadwood boosters smiled as they saw two lines racing to their town. The Elkhorn arrived in December 1890, followed closely by the Burlington in January 1891.[3] Mayor Sol Star summarized the local sentiment, proclaiming that the railroads had finally made Deadwood a "city of permanence" and opened a new age of prosperity.[4] Unfortunately for Minnesela residents, the Elkhorn would bypass their town.

Seth Bullock played only a minor role in attracting the railroads to Deadwood, but he did try to facilitate their entry and profit by their arrival. As the rail lines approached, property values rose dramatically, and a new round of speculation hit town. "The stock excitement of '86 is surpassed by the furore in real estate circles," a Deadwood newspaper proclaimed in 1890.[5] Bullock and Star held a number of pieces of property, and they sold some of their land at inflated prices. In other instances, however, they transferred lots to Miller for only one dollar each. Miller needed the ground for the Deadwood Central, and Bullock and Star's generosity reflected their desire to get that line and the Burlington into town. Bullock also showed his confidence in Deadwood's future by planning a new subdivision, which he called Englewood, situated about one mile out of town on the Sturgis road. The plat of Englewood showed twelve blocks with as many as sixteen lots per block. Bullock named the streets after trees, such as Walnut, Chestnut, and Cedar. Although seemingly well planned, Bullock's subdivision never materialized, perhaps sitting too far out of town.[6]

While Bullock and Star played a small part in assisting the Burlington, they worked more vigorously on behalf of the Elkhorn's arrival. In this case, they challenged Miller's plans. As he laid out the Deadwood Central's right-of-way, Miller acquired much of the land around Deadwood suitable for railroad construction, and some of it blocked the Elkhorn's proposed route. To Bullock, Star, and Harris Franklin, it looked like Miller wanted a Deadwood Central/Burlington monopoly, something they opposed. The three men saw that the only ground available for the Elkhorn's right-of-way was in the channel of Whitewood Creek, and they wanted the city council to narrow the creek's watercourse to twenty-five feet with a second bulkhead. The reclaimed land would serve as the Elkhorn's right-of-way. Miller protested, reminding the council that after the 1883 flood, they had agreed on a fifty-foot channel. With Mayor Star's support, the council voted for a bulkhead that reduced the waterway to forty-five feet, allowing just enough space for the Elkhorn's track. While undoubtedly resolved for the good of Deadwood, the debate brought such acrimony that the paper headlined the story "Railroad War."[7]

While Bullock primarily watched as the railroads built

into Deadwood, he was much more involved as the Elkhorn constructed its line north towards Minnesela. Since the founding of that town in 1881, Bullock had had an ambiguous relationship with its residents. They occupied the open range and offered unwanted competition to Sol Star's flour mill in Deadwood. The rift between Bullock and the Minnesela promoters grew wider when the Medora to Deadwood stage line bypassed their town and Bullock created DeMores. But with the failure of those ventures, the relationship improved. By the time the Elkhorn announced its extension out of Whitewood, the people of Minnesela again trusted Bullock. The town created a board of trade, which distributed promotional literature proclaiming Minnesela as the natural focus of all railroad construction. When it came time to influence the Elkhorn's route, the board looked to Bullock to help sway the railroad. He agreed to assist Minnesela, but he did not guarantee anything.[8]

By 1890, Bullock needed a new enterprise to redeem his economic fortunes, and as a seasoned speculator and promoter, he was a consummate opportunist. When he met with railroad officials, he did not discuss the advantages of Minnesela; instead, he offered them what they wanted: cheap land. In this case, the inducement was a right-of-way across the S & B Stock Farm and property near the old site of DeMores. The Minnesela boosters may have dreamed of attracting the railroad, but the Elkhorn and its subsidiary, the Pioneer Townsite Company, planned to develop their own property and snatched up Bullock's offer. The townsite company had already established a number of communities along the eastern edge of the Black Hills, including Buffalo Gap, Hermosa, and Whitewood, profiting from lot sales in these station stops. When the railroad's route became public, the people of Minnesela were shocked. From their point of view, Bullock had double-crossed them, sacrificing their community for his own personal gain.[9] Local people called the former lawman a "black traitor," but Bullock wasted no time on remorse.[10] He was a frontier capitalist, doing what he could to profit.

The railroad officials worked with Bullock because he could provide land. By this time, he and Star probably controlled nearly two thousand acres around the Belle Fourche River, and Bullock granted a one hundred-foot wide strip across it for the railroad's right-of-way at no charge. More importantly, Bullock offered to sell about one hundred twenty acres south of the Belle Fourche River, just west of its confluence with the Redwater River, to the townsite company for just one dollar. With these generous conditions, Bullock finally got the development he had long sought in the cattle country. The Pioneer Townsite Company would use the acreage for its new townsite of Belle Fourche, and since Bullock and Star still held much of the land around it, they naturally planned to profit from further land sales. Some accounts state that the Elkhorn initially planned to build to Minnesela, but greedy speculators anticipated the railroad's route and claimed the best ground, offering it at inflated prices. While these stories may have some basis in fact, Bullock's actions preempted any other consideration.[11]

Beyond the land offer, Bullock and Star used a couple of other tactics to draw the railroad to the S & B Stock Farm. In the first case, Bullock knew that company officials wanted to build cattle pens. Consequently, he directed them to an open area just west of his ranch. Settlers had not yet occupied this land, but more importantly, this flat expanse was north of the Belle Fourche River. As Bullock explained, most cattle herds roamed on the north side of the river, and cattlemen did not want to drive their animals across it for shipment. This logic was another strike against Minnesela as it sat well south of the Belle Fourche River. Star's political influence also appeared to play a part in the railroad's ultimate decision. As mentioned, the Elkhorn had needed Star's help to get a right-of-way through Deadwood. The reports are jumbled, but Star apparently made it evident to railroad officials that his assistance in Deadwood was contingent upon them working with Bullock to establish a station on the S & B ranch. It may be true, for Star helped get the Elkhorn through Deadwood, and Bullock got the town that he had long desired.[12]

The Elkhorn completed the twenty-two-mile extension from Whitewood to the S & B Stock Farm in August 1890, over four months before the railroad reached Deadwood. Few cheered its arrival. Belle Fourche consisted of little more than some shacks and a few saloons, and the first trains carried no passengers, just cattle. The station opened in December 1890, and the actual town's founding came in July 1891 when the Pioneer Townsite Company began selling lots.[13]

As the townsite company prepared for its July land sale, Bullock held a horse auction in anticipation of losing some of his range. To publicize the event and the subsequent town-lot sale, Bullock and the company started a newspaper, the *Belle Fourche Bee*. Publishing from a partially completed building, the *Bee* flooded the Black Hills with announcements of the sale. To guarantee a large crowd, Bullock also provided transportation incentives. He offered to refund the train fare to any person who bought a horse; he convinced the Elkhorn to reduce transportation charges for any horse costing over a thousand dollars; and he got the railroad to run special trains.[14]

The publicity and promotions, however, did not bring the sale Bullock wanted. While the five-day event saw a number of people attend, sales and prices proved uninspiring. Bullock reportedly wanted to sell 425 horses, but he sold less than 250. Most of the animals went for between $50 and $400 each, moving the *Black Hills Daily Times* to comment that the same quality of horses in Kentucky would have brought from $500 to $2,500. Bullock's grandson stated some years later that the auction brought $55,000, but estimates gained from newspaper articles indicate something closer to $30,000.[15] No matter what the sale returned, its revenue, as well as what came from his business dealings in the Belle Fourche area, greatly enhanced Bullock's financial situation. After all the frustrations of the 1880s, he finally had a venture pay off. As banker R. E. Driscoll reported, these activities allowed Bullock to get "back on his feet financially."[16]

A few weeks after the horse sale, the Pioneer Townsite Company held a town-lot auction. Whenever the company created a town near an existing one, it offered free lots to businesses willing to move. This step ensured an immediate business district while undermining an established locale like Minnesela. The company had done the same thing at Buffalo Gap and Whitewood. After the businessmen selected their lots, company officials sold the rest at auction. Minnesela residents fumed, demanding a station. To make their point, they routed their freight through Deadwood, using the Burlington Railroad. Some physically tried to block Minnesela businesses from relocating, while others disrupted the bidding at the land auction.[17]

Despite the opposition, Belle Fourche gained momentum. As businesses moved from Minnesela, the townsite company built a two-story hotel, and Star and Bullock opened a hardware store. The nearby stock pens proved their worth as cattle shipments skyrocketed, and the cowboys spent their time off in Belle Fourche, quickly turning it into a cow town. Described as wide-open and brawling, Belle Fourche offered cowboys and cowmen whatever they wanted on "saloon street," now Fifth Avenue. Bullock's impressions of the town went unrecorded, but he may have appreciated the atmosphere. He enjoyed drinking, sometimes to excess, and the rowdiness may have reminded him of the Wild West days. By the 1890s, the frontier era had nearly ended, and this raw new town was one of its last vestiges.[18]

Railroads, cattle pens, and businesses did not, however, guarantee permanence. Minnesela still had the county seat, which the residents of Belle Fourche wanted. When Butte County voters had a chance to move it in 1892, Minnesela prevailed, but Bullock would not let that happen again. He took the lead in raising two thousand dollars for a Butte County courthouse and in having it constructed in Belle Fourche by 1894. When it came time for another vote, Bullock reportedly brought in men from Black Hills mining camps and recruited people from Wyoming and Montana, promising them liquor and a good time. He had built a racetrack just west of town, and he sponsored races there the day before the election. This combination of tactics brought a crowd to the polls in 1894, and Belle Fourche carried the day.[19]

Legend has it that the electoral victory inspired some Belle Fourche partisans to take immediate action. Under the cover of darkness, they rode into Minnesela, ransacked the makeshift courthouse, removed the county records, and carried them back to Belle Fourche. The next day the Butte County sheriff formed a posse to retrieve the documents, and as they rode into Belle Fourche, violence seemed assured. But at the critical moment, Belle Fourche supporters turned over the papers, accepting the fact that they would have to wait until 1 January 1895, the designated date for the transfer.[20] Late in life, Bullock's son Stanley reflected on the Minnesela raid and commented that the story had probably been "exaggerated," but he offered no details as to what he meant.[21] The story, however, is reminiscent of the county-seat fights that went on throughout the West.

From 1879 to 1894, Bullock had speculated on several business enterprises, and the creation of Belle Fourche had led to his economic recovery after some spectacular losses. Throughout those fifteen years, Bullock still found time for his most fundamental interests: family, politics, and friends. In 1880, Bullock and Martha had had their last child, a son named Stanley. While this third child completed the Bullocks' immediate family, the couple also took care of other children at various times. For instance, a nephew, Douglas Kislingbury, the son of Seth's late sister, spent time with them. He came to Deadwood when his father, Lieutenant Frederick F. Kislingbury, went on military assignment. In the style of the nineteenth-century business class, Martha raised her children with the aid of a servant and provided a rich environment for her family. She sang, joined organizations, and promoted education. Several choral events in the northern Hills featured the talents of Mrs. Bullock, as well as those of her two daughters. She also belonged to societies such as the Culture Club and founded a literary group known as the Round Table Club. A former schoolteacher, Martha Bullock promoted education, helping establish public schools in Deadwood. Because of her gender, however, she could not serve on the governing board. Instead, the city council selected her husband for the board of education in 1883. Bullock held this position for over a decade, hiring teachers and selecting curriculum.[22]

Bullock's time with the board of education reflected his ongoing interest in politics. While losses in 1877 and 1878 convinced him to avoid running for major office again, he did work behind the scenes, campaigning for candidates and attending Republican conventions. Bullock traveled to Vermillion, Fargo, Pierre, and Watertown for territorial gatherings and to Chicago and Nashville for national conventions during the 1880s. From time to time, Republican allies promoted him as a possible candidate for higher office. Representatives from Lawrence County nominated him for congressional delegate at the Republican territorial convention in 1888, for example. East-River Republicans, however, disagreed, and the convention chose another man.

In local affairs, Bullock fought the influence of the Lead City-based Homestake Mining Company, which, many suspected, bought off government officials. At times, he joined Republican groups known as the "Anti-Homestake Faction" and the "mugwumps," who were trying to keep a political balance between Lead City and Deadwood. No matter the fight, however, Bullock relished his role as a leading Republican in Dakota Territory and then South Dakota.[23]

Through his years in business and politics, Bullock made a number of acquaintances, but he had a special affinity for those he saw as fellow pioneers. As Deadwood's first decade came to an end in 1886, Bullock and sixty other "old timers" gathered to organize what they called the Pioneers of '76. While this first effort stalled, they successfully established the Society of the Black Hills Pioneers in 1889. The group's official goals included collecting information on the area's early settlement, gathering biographies of Black Hills founders, and helping pioneers who had fallen on hard times.[24] Bullock, however, saw the organization in a more celebratory light. He considered himself and his associates to be trailblazers who, he wrote, had led the way "for the march of the Nation's progress."[25] Determined to highlight their achievements, Bullock served as president of the society in 1890 and 1891, and in 1892 he coordinated the annual excursion. Bullock saw no greater accomplishment than the founding of Belle Fourche, and he took his fellow pioneers and families there for their summer outing.[26]

Just as Bullock drew his old friends more closely around him, he and Sol Star ended their partnership. Throughout much of the 1880s, Bullock and Star had developed different interests. While Bullock spent time trying to make the Iron Hill Company a success, Star focused on running the Deadwood flouring mill. Then as Bullock kept his political ambitions behind the scenes, Star won a number of elections, serving as Deadwood's mayor from 1884 to 1893 and representing Lawrence County in the state legislature in the early 1890s. Their mutual investments in Star & Bullock Hardware and the S & B Ranch kept the partnership together, but Bullock's speculative ventures kept their operations in financial trouble and put a strain on their relationship. As they missed tax payments and avoided bills, the two men sought solutions. Finally, the horse sale and development of Belle Fourche brought some relief and provided the opportunity to dissolve the partnership. In 1893, Star began selling his interests in the hardware store to Bullock, and early the next year, he transferred his land holdings along the Belle Fourche River. After eighteen years of working together, the men ended their partnership in 1894. Bullock and Star would remain friends.[27]

Ironically, as Star and Bullock drifted apart, Bullock encountered a man whom he came to idolize: Theodore Roosevelt. Misinterpretations and Bullock's tendency to tell romanticized tales have caused some confusion as to when and how these two men met. As he grew older, Bullock liked to recount tales of the old days, and in particular, he enjoyed stories that drew Roosevelt into the narrative. Both he and Roosevelt told the story that Roosevelt, serving as deputy sheriff of Billings County in northern Dakota Territory, arrested a horse thief that Bullock wanted as well. Some authors extrapolated from these accounts that the two men met then, possibly in 1884 or 1886.[28]

A careful reading shows, however, that Roosevelt and Bullock actually met later. In letters to John Hay and to his son Kermit, Roosevelt clearly stated that he first met Bullock in 1892.[29] In that year, Roosevelt, who was serving as a federal civil service commissioner, traveled from his old ranch near Medora to Deadwood en route to the Sioux reservations. When Roosevelt and his companions crossed the Belle Fourche River, they encountered a cautious Bullock. As Roosevelt admitted, his party looked out of place, "exactly like an outfit of tinhorn gamblers." Once they exchanged introductions, Bullock became much more cordial, and when he heard about Roosevelt's occupation, he remarked: "Well, anything civil goes with me." This simple meeting initiated what would become a lifelong friendship between Roosevelt and Bullock.[30]

At the time, however, Roosevelt did not apparently mean much to Bullock. But once the commissioner made it to Deadwood, a group of Republicans demanded that he be their guest of honor. They escorted him to the Deadwood Opera House, and there, as Roosevelt later recalled, he "was forced to open the campaign" for President Benjamin Harrison's reelection.[31] Throughout the swirl of events, Bullock played no obvious part.[32] He may have remained on the northern range, where he had met Roosevelt's party, or he may have discounted the civil service commissioner as a passing dandy. No matter, Bullock would never again ignore Roosevelt's comings and goings.

By 1894, Bullock had seemingly set a new course. One of his speculative ventures had finally paid off, and his financial standing had improved. He had ended his long-term partnership with Star, and he had become the primary owner of the S & B Ranch and Star & Bullock Hardware. Based on these long-term businesses, Bullock could seemingly anticipate some economic stability, but it was not to be. In March 1894, a fire started across the street from Star & Bullock Hardware and spread down Main Street, destroying much of lower Deadwood. The fire consumed the front of Bullock's building, but his fireproof, which contained the majority of his inventory, survived. As he surveyed the damage, Bullock told the reporter from the *Times* that he had been "burned and smoked out so many times that he feels much like a smoked ham."[33] But disasters did not stop there. Eighteen months later, in September 1895, a fire wiped out much of Belle Fourche's business district.[34]

The fires again set Bullock back financially, and they marked the end of Bullock's entrepreneurial leadership. While he would reopen the Star & Bullock Hardware in Deadwood, and he would again invest in Belle Fourche, he would no longer be a driving force in either town. As one observer commented, with the fire, "Belle Fourche lost its identity as a Bullock promotion." As the residents rebuilt, they developed a new community spirit, separate from the Bullock legacy.[35]

For fifteen years after the Deadwood fire of 1879, Bullock worked to make himself wealthy and the northern Black Hills prosperous, and he partially succeeded. By 1895, Deadwood had entered into a new era of economic development: ore-processing plants had opened, railroads had built in, and businesses had grown up. While Bullock did not make as much money as he might have liked, his unwavering support helped ensure Deadwood's ultimate success. He could also look at Belle Fourche with pride. Here was a town he fostered and a place in which he profited, a success that came just in the nick of time.

By the 1890s, the possibility of new ventures bringing windfall profits had diminished. The northern Black Hills had matured economically. Most speculative opportunities had been fully exploited, and Bullock realized that times had changed. With the advent of the railroads, Deadwood and the Black Hills had become integrated into national business trends and into the policies of the federal government. In this environment, Bullock would again step forward to play a prominent role to help connect the region with the nation. He would return to civic leadership and only occasionally seek out new investments. Instead, he sought the satisfaction and stability that came with public service.

PUBLIC
SERVANT
1895–1919

7

Moving to a National Stage

The fifty cowboys put on a show that all in Washington would remember. As they rode down Pennsylvania Avenue, they weaved their horses back and forth, shouting "Whoopee!" and "Rah for Teddy." At times they paused to salute a pretty girl or lasso an unsuspecting child. Each man played his part to the hilt. Some wore sheepskin chaps, and others had on leather breeches. From their belts hung six shooters, making the riders look like classic western cowhands. They had come to salute Theodore Roosevelt in the 1905 inaugural parade, and leading them down the street and reveling in the glory was Seth Bullock. He had organized the troop, brought them to Washington, and led them in this celebration for his friend.[1] According to one account, Bullock's men were "the hit of the whole show," with only Roosevelt's Rough Riders gaining more attention.[2]

In 1876, Bullock had led the Helena Fire Department in a parade celebrating the nation's centennial. Twenty-nine years later, he directed his "Company of Cowboys" as they honored the president. During the intervening years, Bullock had taken on many roles, from lawman to speculator, but this event in the country's capital marked his ascension onto the national stage. He was no longer just a local leader; instead, Bullock was a trusted confidant of a president. The roots of this transformation came when Bullock met Roosevelt in 1892, but Bullock's climb to the larger arena started during the Spanish-American War. Both Roosevelt and Bullock volunteered to fight, and while they had entirely different experiences, they left the war respecting one another. This connection allowed Bullock to change his life again. He would return to public service, but this time he would represent the federal government within the Black Hills and South Dakota.

In the wake of the 1894 and 1895 Deadwood and Belle Fourche fires, Bullock stepped back from his business interests, seemingly unable to determine what to do next. These catastrophes reversed his earlier financial gains, and throughout the remainder of the decade, he struggled with debt. He failed to pay creditors, avoided paying property taxes, and watched as some of his property was sold at fore-closure sales. But when Deadwood resident William Remer asked him about his problems in 1896, Bullock responded that he "will pull through," reflecting his usual confidence and his faith in overcoming hard times.[3] But, the former lawman had no idea how he was going to turn his fortunes around. He still had ties to the hardware business, the ranch, and the mining industry, but in the years immediately after the fires, he lacked the desire or the money to do much with any of them.[4]

The hardware store's brick fireproof had survived the 1894 calamity, but it took Bullock nearly a year to begin rebuilding the destroyed storefront. Then once construction got underway, he changed his mind and decided to erect a hotel instead. Bullock modified his plans because he envisioned a much smaller hardware store, which would require less capital and less attention to construct and operate. A downsized retail business would free up space at the corner of Main and Wall for another enterprise, and the city needed a hotel. Bullock reasoned that local boosters and outside investors would provide enough of the financing to build a hotel, allowing him to reconstruct his hardware store on the profits.

Deadwood promoters had long desired a "first-class hotel building." When the Deadwood Board of Trade initially met in 1881, the members talked about constructing a hotel that reflected a modern urban center.[5] While Deadwood already had hotels, most catered to single working men who lived there permanently, and visitors often described the facilities as rundown or dilapidated. The board of trade failed to get a hotel in 1881, and the discussions continued throughout the decade. In 1891, as the railroads arrived in town, the board tried again with Bullock chairing the committee. They contacted hotel entrepreneurs and started gathering subscriptions to underwrite the cost. After one developer backed out, a local investment group stepped forward and organized the Deadwood Hotel Company. They acquired a site at the corner of Main and Shine streets, excavated a basement, and poured the foundations. The developers had reportedly spent nearly fifty thousand dollars when the project abruptly ended. The financial panic of 1893 stifled further investment, and the work was abandoned.[6]

Three years after the Deadwood Hotel Company stopped its project, Bullock came up with his own plan. In light of the earlier fiasco, Bullock offered a much more limited proposition. He wanted the local citizens to buy the lot that joined his Main Street property to the south and give it to him. Here he would build his new, smaller hardware store and look for investors to build a hotel at his former business location. To sell the community on his proposition, he convinced the local newspaper that a hotel on that corner "would enhance the value of every lot in that part of town and the owners can well afford to raise the bonus asked."[7] To ease their concerns over another failed hotel project, Bullock offered a "guaranty bond" to assure the completion of the enterprise.[8]

The citizens of Deadwood agreed. They raised six thousand dollars for the lot and passed it on to Bullock. With the location for his store guaranteed, Bullock formed the Bullock Hotel Company and began construction, using sandstone from Boulder Park for the building's front. He, however, lacked the resources to finish the hotel on his own. In early 1896, W. W. Marsh and Fred Evans, Jr., agreed to complete the project. These men had hotel connections in Hot Springs and Omaha, and they formed the Dakota Hotel Company to run their new Deadwood business.[9] As they took charge, the newspaper anxiously covered their progress. It described the furniture Evans purchased in Chicago as the "finest and handsomest" manufactured, and the "splendid style" of the barber shop and Turkish baths in the basement as an "elegant" luxury.[10] When the facility opened in April 1896, Deadwood residents celebrated. Their desire for a fully modern hotel had finally been achieved.[11]

To what extent Bullock remained involved is a mystery. Once Evans took over, Bullock's name stayed on the building but was never again associated with the hotel's operation. Managers and proprietors would come and go, and Bullock apparently had no say. A group of Deadwood businessmen, including D. A. McPherson, N. E. Franklin, and George Ayres, eventually took control of the Dakota Hotel Company's board of directors, but Bullock was not involved. When George Ayres acquired the building in 1904, he bought it from a Deadwood bank. Bullock apparently started the ball rolling, got his name on the hotel, and then severed his connection.[12]

As the hotel went up, Bullock built a one-story structure for his hardware store on the adjoining lot. The building was much smaller than his former location, and reports circulated that a second story would soon be added, but Bullock never contracted for the extra work. In fact, the reopened Star & Bullock Hardware seemingly did little business at its new location, known as the Bullock Annex. The company immediately fell delinquent on its property taxes, and by 1898, Bullock was negotiating to sell his remaining interest.[13] In 1900, the Deadwood paper reported that the remainder of Star & Bullock's stock, "consisting mainly of shelf hardware," had been sold.[14] Not long after, the Bullock Hotel extended its operations into the annex.[15] With the hardware store's closing, Bullock's days as a merchant had come to an end.

Bullock also became less involved with his ranch in the mid-1890s. He sold a number of cattle, and rumors persistently circulated that he was selling his land. Bullock, however, retained possession, and in the early twentieth century, his son Stanley moved to Belle Fourche to manage the Bullock Land and Cattle Company and to open a real-estate and insurance office. Through the years, the younger Bullock sold ranch property to an expanding Belle Fourche market. Despite Seth Bullock's diminished involvement, the S & B Ranch continued to operate, and he still visited periodically, especially during the planting season.[16]

While he was reducing his role at the store and on the ranch, Bullock maintained a presence in the mining industry. In fact, the publisher of the 1898 *Deadwood City Directory* listed Bullock's occupation as "mining." Yet, when compared to his previous mining ventures, his late nineteenth-century activities were small. Bullock no longer had an interest in the Iron Hill property, but he still held claims in the Galena silver district and in the Bald Mountain gold district. He did little with them, however. Poor silver prices prevented any development at Galena, and Bullock seemed to lack the desire to develop his Bald Mountain holdings. By this time, a new cyanide process offered hope for treating the area's refractory ores, and news stories connected Bullock with the construction of a cyanide plant at Central City. Before any production was recorded, however, Bullock sold his Bald Mountain claims.[17]

Bullock displayed more interest in mining when prospectors established the Ragged Top Mining District in 1896. Located four miles west of Carbonate Camp, this gold discovery stimulated another rush. By the end of the year, mining men had moved in and the towns of Balmoral and Preston had formed. General Green B. Raum, a Chicago promoter and investor, joined the excitement, and with the assistance of Bullock, he purchased the Gold Belt and Alaska claims, organized the town of Ragged Top, just north of Balmoral and Preston, and created the Elk Springs Water Company. While Raum worked as president and treasurer of these ventures, Bullock served as vice-president. How Raum and Bullock met is unknown, but Raum probably recruited Bullock because of his reputation and experience. He counted on Bullock to manage his affairs when he traveled to Chicago.[18]

Ragged Top had but a brief existence. Just weeks after announcing his plans, Raum left for home, telling a newspaper reporter that he would return shortly with his family. In his absence, Bullock tried to advance his interests, but the Ragged Top ore played out just below the surface. Bullock brought in a diamond drill to explore more deeply, but he found little of value. By the summer of 1897, the Ragged Top excitement had collapsed, and Raum never returned. While some mining continued, any hopes of a prolonged and profitable boom were gone.[19]

Just as Bullock stepped back from mining, ranching, and retail in the late nineteenth century, he also stepped back from community boosterism. Where Bullock had been the driving force behind the Deadwood Board of Trade in 1881, when a similar organization formed in 1897, he played no part. When a committee met to discuss the 1898 Omaha Exposition, he was again absent. By contrast, his former partner, Sol Star, participated in both. Bullock even disappeared from politics, ignoring the 1896 election. Bullock's only apparent venture into community affairs came when he joined a sheriff's posse to hunt for bank robbers who had escaped from the Deadwood jail in 1897. Bullock always enjoyed law enforcement, and this adventure probably reminded him of his days as sheriff. It may also have convinced him to seek out more action and leave the staid life of a businessman behind forever.[20]

Bullock's chance for excitement came with the Spanish-American War. As war talk between Spain and America over Cuban freedom heated up in the early months of 1898, many people wanted to expand the army. In particular, politicians in Colorado, Wyoming, and South Dakota proposed organizing volunteer cavalry units, or "troops of cowboys," which would bring "bravery, loyalty, hardiness, and horsemanship" to the fray.[21] Once war came in April 1898, Congress agreed, and it passed a measure that created a volunteer infantry force of one hundred twenty-five thousand and authorized three cavalry regiments specifically from the Rocky Mountain and Great Plains states. Secretary of War Russell A. Alger organized the three troops, known as the First, Second, and Third United States Volunteer Cavalry Regiments, and selected their commanders. For the First Regiment, he chose Theodore Roosevelt. Working as the assistant secretary of the navy, Roosevelt made it well known that he wanted to fight and that his western connections would allow him to find the necessary fighting men. Roosevelt, however, asked that Leonard Wood lead his unit while he gained more experience as second in command. For the Second Regiment, Alger picked Judge Jay L. Torrey, a prominent Wyoming politician, and for the Third, he named Melvin B. Grigsby, South Dakota's attorney general. Both of these men had fighting experience and had recently been in Washington promoting the legislation that allowed for the cowboy units.[22]

As word spread, the nation's newspapers began applying nicknames to the western cowboy troops. For instance, the *Denver Republican* headlined a story with "Regiments of Western Sharpshooters and Cowboy Rough Riders," initially referring to all the cavalrymen as "rough riders."[23] But soon more specific nicknames appeared. The First Cavalry unit gained such alliterative names as "Wood's Wild Westerners," to be replaced by "Teddy's Terrors," "Teddy's Texas Tarantulas," and "Teddy's Riotous Rounders," with "Roosevelt's Rough Riders" emerging as the favorite. Roosevelt himself did not approve of the names. He wanted the troops known as "mounted riflemen," but he eventually accepted the Rough Rider label. In the meantime, the Second Volunteer unit became known as Torrey's Rocky Mountain Riders, and the Third was called Grigsby's Cowboys.[24]

Recently commissioned as a colonel, Grigsby arrived in Sioux Falls with orders to break his regiment into twelve troops, with five coming from South Dakota and the remainder from Nebraska, North Dakota, and Montana.[25] Grigsby, who appointed captains to recruit and organize the individual troops, needed men with solid reputations and proven ability to lead. For Troop A, he selected Seth Bullock. Going back to his years as Deadwood's first sheriff, Bullock had the experience and the qualities Grigsby wanted. More importantly, Bullock was well connected and "universally respected."[26] By the end of May, Grigsby's officers had organized his regiment of nearly a thousand men.[27]

As these events unfolded, Bullock watched with excitement. As a boy, he wanted to fight in the Civil War. When he worked as sheriff and deputy marshal, he found a job he was good at. With the Spanish-American War, he saw his chance to return to his natural calling. When he heard about the cowboy units, he told William Remer that if he got a "commission he would go to war—that he was bred that way."[28] When Grigsby made him a captain and put him in charge of Troop A, Bullock promptly went to work. He opened recruiting offices in Lead and Deadwood, and in five days he signed up his allotment of eighty-four men, and still more wanted to volunteer. The majority of Troop A came from Deadwood, Lead, and Terry. Ironically, of the eighty-four recruits, only twenty-two listed their occupation as cowboys, while thirty-six were miners. On 8 May, the men arrived at Fort Meade and were mustered into service.[29]

While Bullock was fifty-one years old when he received his commission, his contemporaries still described him as "muscular and as straight as an arrow, a magnificent type of the far western soldier."[30] Yet, he failed his physical examination. Whatever problem he had went unrecorded, and it did not prevent him from serving. A historian of the regiment noted, "The captain was at first refused upon a slight technicality by the medical examiners."[31] In the opinion of William Remer, Bullock's political allies, particularly United States Senators Richard F. Pettigrew and James H. Kyle, fixed the exam results.[32] Whatever happened, Bullock soon joined his men at Fort Meade, where they trained while waiting for orders to depart.

After two weeks at the fort, Troops A, C, and D boarded a train for Chickamauga, Georgia. With Troop C from Belle Fourche and Troop D out of Sturgis, the three groups were collectively known as "Grigsby's Black Hills Cowboys."[33] The nearly two hundred fifty men could barely restrain their enthusiasm as they headed east. The volunteers saw themselves as true Americans, hardened and transformed by the frontier experience, and were confident that they could easily defeat the Spanish. Crowds along their route reinforced their exuberance and pride. Whenever the train stopped, people cheered, bands played, and food appeared. The cowboys responded with "whoops" and cheers, and a Chicago correspondent reported: "Better representatives of the wild and woolly west could not be found anywhere. All of them are veterans of the plains and inured to the hardships of frontier life, which fact renders them peculiarly useful in the present war."[34]

They arrived at Camp Thomas at Chickamauga about 1 June, and there they stayed. The camp had around forty thousand men, and while they waited for horses, uniforms, and orders, they drilled. Camp life proved to be hot, unhealthy, and boring. A few of the volunteers wrote letters to Deadwood newspapers, often highlighting their troops' virtues while denigrating the infantrymen they were forced to camp with. For example, when Bullock's men saw some soldiers harassing women from the Salvation Army, the cowboys, as they called themselves, roughed up the offenders and "escorted the ladies to the train to see that no further insult was offered."[35] Another letter home stated that Grigsby's "Rough Riders are showing themselves superior in every respect, and they are becoming familiarly known as the crack regiment of the park."[36]

Correspondents commented frequently on Bullock and his actions as troop commander. In a letter written soon after arriving at Chickamauga, a trooper reported, "Captain Bullock is easily the most popular man in the camp and is much sought after by everyone, and with his own troop there is no one who can equal him."[37] Some of Bullock's popularity came from his prior notoriety. Papers from Washington, D.C., to Chattanooga, Tennessee, ran embellished accounts of Bullock's exploits in Helena and Deadwood, describing him as "one of the best known men of the northwest," a true fighter and a terror "to the evil-doers of the early days."[38] His own men liked him because he always had a good word for them and stuck up for them when necessary. And they repaid the kindness. When Bullock fell ill and wanted milk, some of his men sneaked out of camp and found a nearby herd of cows. Bullock reportedly commented, "Stolen milk, like stolen fruit, is a very superior article."[39] When Bullock had to leave camp for a quick trip to Deadwood, he returned to the cheers of his men, who greeted him like a "long lost brother."[40]

Beyond the normal camp activities, Captain Bullock had an opportunity to display the characteristics that made him a successful frontier sheriff. When payday came in early July, the camp's infantry soldiers went to nearby Chattanooga, Tennessee, to celebrate, and on two consecutive days, fights erupted. Each time, Bullock stepped forward to quell the disturbance. During the first affray, Bullock grabbed two of the most quarrelsome men, turned them over to some of his cowboys, and ordered the rest of the brawlers to disburse. His rapid action and stern words quieted the affair, at least for that night. When the combatants returned the next day, Bullock "threatened to turn all hell and the cowboys loose on them in a minute if quiet was not restored."[41] He quickly arrested a few and sent them to jail. With violence still imminent, Bullock, with the approval of the chief, took control of the city's police department. One correspondent reported that Bullock risked his life and limb as he arrested troublemakers, but in less than five hours he had the city "as quiet and peaceful as Deadwood upon a Sunday night." In the end, the chief of police thanked Bullock publicly, and Colonel Grigsby sent his compliments.[42]

Aside from breaking up fights on payday, Bullock found life at Camp Thomas as boring as his men did, but he had a variety of activities that kept him busy. Bullock performed military duties, such as checking supplies and ordering equipment. The army had supplied his troop with animals, but Bullock thought the horses were of poor quality. He wanted new ones, and to make his case, he brought a superior officer to the picket line. While looking at one of the horses, the officer asked Bullock, "What's the matter with that animal?" Invoking his dry wit, Bullock responded, "That horse; he's an immune." When asked to explain, Bullock said, "Why, he can't catch anything."[43] At other times, Bullock and his men entertained themselves with sports. Once during target practice, the captain and Major Leigh H. French, his immediate superior, got into a shooting match. Bullock prevailed, and that evening Troop A smoked cigars at the major's expense. Bullock also did some touring, taking a trip to Lookout Mountain in Tennessee, where he acquired a hand-carved gavel inscribed with "Lookout Mt." He sent it to Mayor Sol Star, with the instructions that he and all future mayors of Deadwood should use it.[44]

As camp life dragged on, the Black Hills men became disenchanted. By August, the war appeared over, and as they heard about the glories of Roosevelt's Rough Riders, Grigsby's Cowboys felt discriminated against and abused. They wanted to go home. Some of the volunteers circulated a petition protesting their prolonged stay in Georgia, and the protest resulted in their arrest. Bullock, however, interceded and freed them from the guardhouse. Although he reprimanded the men strongly, he agreed with their sentiments. Finally, after three months at Camp Thomas, the men began their trip home.[45] Their friends in Deadwood planned a grand celebration, but instead of arriving all at once, the troops came in piecemeal, muting any ovation. Besides, few of the returning men wanted to celebrate. They were too "disgusted over the fact that they were kept from going to the front."[46]

Many of the Black Hills volunteers saw their war service as a waste of time, but it remade Bullock's life. It gave him the direction he was lacking, and it became as important to him as any previous experience, with the exception of his time as sheriff. From 1898 on, everything Bullock did built upon his military service. Part of his changed fortunes derived from greater notoriety. The national newspapers had described Bullock as a man of the frontier, a no-nonsense pioneer, and this celebrity status endured. Over the next several years, the eastern press continued to run articles that aggrandized Bullock's past, often describing him as "a foe to the Indian and the desperado" and claiming that "he shot himself into fame."[47] A cigar maker in Maine labeled a line of cigars the "Seth Bullock" brand, perhaps paying the highest honor to this former sheriff, businessman, and rising western hero.[48]

Similarly, the war earned Bullock a new measure of respect at home. From the end of his service until his death, he used the title of "captain," and because he had comported himself well during his brief enlistment, most in Deadwood considered him deserving of the honor. With his new stature, Bullock took on the role of local military leader. When Civil War veterans held a Grand Army of the Republic encampment at Hot Springs in June 1899, Bullock led a detachment of his Black Hills volunteers to the gathering, telling his men, "In honoring them we honor ourselves."[49] Four months later, a detachment of Black Hills men who had fought in the Filipino Insurrection returned home. A parade celebrated their arrival in Deadwood, with Bullock commanding a troop of "Grigsby's rough riders."[50]

In the years after the war, Bullock seemed willing to make public appearances only if they reflected his new role. For instance, in early 1901, Bullock recognized that twenty-five years had passed since the founding of Deadwood, and he went before the Society of Black Hills Pioneers to recommend a celebration. The group agreed and asked Bullock to take the lead, but he refused. Instead, others in Deadwood developed a multiday celebration that climaxed on July Fourth. Bullock did participate in the festivities, but in ways that highlighted his military status. When troops arrived from Fort Meade, Bullock rode out to escort them into town, and when the committee asked him to serve as grand marshal for the Fourth of July parade, Bullock proudly did so, wearing his captain's uniform.[51]

While the Spanish-American War increased Bullock's stature and gave him a new public persona, it also cemented his friendship with Theodore Roosevelt. Roosevelt's successful Cuban campaign had been much in the news, adding further frustration to the stateside travails of the other two volunteer cavalry regiments. When Roosevelt returned home and started celebrating his group's achievements, he occasionally invited men from the other cavalry units, including Bullock, to join his Rough Riders. Bullock had to have been flattered, and when Roosevelt entered national politics, the captain became all the more awestruck by a man he considered a kindred spirit. As Roosevelt's son Kermit reported some years later: "Seth Bullock was a hero-worshiper and father was his great hero."[52] For twenty years after the Spanish-American War, Bullock did whatever he could to help Roosevelt, politically and personally, and Roosevelt returned the kindness, accepting Bullock as one of his friends.[53]

The first extended period of time that Roosevelt and Bullock spent together was apparently during the presidential campaign of 1900. As the vice-presidential nominee of William McKinley, Roosevelt traveled west to campaign for the ticket. As a standard campaign technique, he invited Rough Riders to join him. Most of the time their presence just reminded the audience of Roosevelt's wartime heroics, while sometimes they provided protection. In late August, Bullock received a letter inviting him to accompany the candidate on part of his trip. Bullock accepted the offer, joining the train at Yankton, South Dakota. Over the next week, he rode with Roosevelt through eastern South Dakota and then into North Dakota and on to Montana. During this time, Roosevelt and Bullock exchanged stories of the West and established a bond of trust.[54]

At Butte, Montana, Bullock went from a mere traveling companion to Roosevelt's bodyguard. The miners in Butte, who wholeheartedly supported Democratic nominee William Jennings Bryan, were overtly hostile to Roosevelt, and he expected trouble when he gave his speech at the opera house. Instead, the audience listened with fixed attention. Roosevelt initially took some pride in this achievement, convinced that his rhetorical powers had held the audience rapt and precluded interruptions. It surprised him to discover that Bullock had sent word out that if anyone made a noise, he would kill them, and he proceeded to sit on the stage behind Roosevelt, with a gun visible on each hip.[55]

The hostility in Butte outraged Bullock, and with Roosevelt planning a stop in Deadwood, the former lawmen intended to make sure that the candidate would be treated with honor. Ten days before the visit, the paper published a letter from Bullock that spelled out his vision for a successful "non-partisan" stopover. Citizens of all political persuasions needed to work for what he called a "broad gauge affair." He requested a great processional, which would include people from the Hills and cowboys from the ranges, and because the event would be at night, he envisioned a thousand torches lighting the way. He explained the activities in promotional terms, pointing out that reporters from across the nation traveled with Roosevelt. Given a positive impression, they "would advertise the Hills as nothing else could." He emphasized, "You have no idea what it means for the Hills."[56]

When Roosevelt's train rolled into Deadwood at 8 P.M. on 3 October, the residents responded the way Bullock had asked. A large crowd, which included delegations from every northern Hills town, five hundred cowboys, and a women's "Rough Rider Glee Club," met the candidate at the North Western Railroad freight station in lower Deadwood. Amidst a deafening roar, the candidate boarded an old stagecoach, and with Bullock in the driver's seat, the entourage escorted the candidate up Main Street and over to the Burlington depot on Sherman Street. Once there, Roosevelt climbed aboard the interurban line and made a quick trip to Lead, speaking before a large crowd in the Miners' Hall and an even larger one outside.

When he returned to Deadwood, another joyous march took him to the Deadwood Opera House. The town glowed as Bullock had foreseen. Electric lights had been strung across the streets, rockets were shot into the night sky, and torches burned everywhere. Observers estimated the crowd at between five and ten thousand, and as his campaign train left three and one-half hours later, Roosevelt could reflect on what was reported as the most excited and demonstrative crowd of his nine-thousand-mile trip.[57] The newspapermen, too, did what Bullock wanted; they gave positive accounts of Deadwood. For instance, the columnist from the Associated Press wrote that he had expected a wilderness, "but it looks more like State street in Chicago."[58]

From this point on, Bullock attached himself firmly to Roosevelt's activities and achievements. When McKinley and Roosevelt won the November election, Bullock helped organize a "Ratification Parade" for Deadwood, serving as chief marshal. After he became president, Roosevelt made another excursion across the nation in 1903. Bullock joined him at Sioux Falls in early April, spending the next two months with Roosevelt as the president crisscrossed the West, stopping at countless towns, including Edgemont, South Dakota, in late April. A large contingent from throughout the Hills greeted him there, and James Conzett, president of the Society of Black Hills Pioneers, took the opportunity to make Roosevelt an honorary member, an action that Bullock had initiated. A little later, Bullock accompanied Roosevelt into Yellowstone Park and then on to Butte, Montana, where they had met a hostile audience three years earlier. In anticipation of trouble, Bullock went to Butte three days ahead of Roosevelt to arrange for a bodyguard. This time, however, the miners were much more cordial, causing Bullock to relax with a few drinks. Much to Roosevelt's horror, Bullock had a few too many, and the president had Bullock turn over his gun. Two years after this extended train trip, Bullock organized his Company of Cowboys for Roosevelt's inaugural parade. Through these encounters, Roosevelt came to accept and respect Bullock as the quintessential American frontiersman.[59]

Roosevelt trusted Bullock enough to have him introduce his sons to the West. In 1903, just two months after his western excursion, Roosevelt sent Theodore Roosevelt, Jr., age sixteen, and George Roosevelt, his nephew, to Deadwood for a two-week stay with Bullock. Two years later, Roosevelt's second son, Kermit, also sixteen, made the first of at least three trips to Bullock's West. The boys learned to ride and shoot at the ranch, and they made a number of horseback trips, checking out good fishing holes and searching for game. The *Custer Chronicle* reported that Kermit killed a "small brown bear" and "three wildcats" during his 1905 visit.[60] The next year, Bullock took Kermit, his own son Stanley, and a few others on a ride to the old Roosevelt ranch near Medora, North Dakota. Bullock hoped to get Roosevelt's third son, Archie, to the West, but Roosevelt confided that Archie had become enamored with sailing, and there just was not enough water in the Black Hills. Yet, in 1910 when Archie reached sixteen, he also made a pilgrimage to South Dakota, and Bullock took him on a tour of the American Indian reservations. Roosevelt's youngest son, Quentin, did not make it to the Hills. The Roosevelt sons who did visit the West greatly valued the experience, especially Kermit who relied on Bullock for advice for many years to come.[61]

Much had changed for Bullock since the fires of 1894 and 1895. Where he had once appeared to have lost purpose, the Spanish-American War and Theodore Roosevelt gave him new direction. But traveling with the president and entertaining his children were just the beginning. Roosevelt also helped Bullock gain federal appointments: forest supervisor in 1901 and United States marshal in 1906. These positions would allow Captain Bullock to assert his leadership abilities and return to activities that suited his talents.

8

A Federal Man

The Spanish-American War brought Bullock to the national stage, a new venue for this Black Hills pioneer. Prior to 1898, Bullock had worked for local progress. From sheriff to town founder, he had labored to bring prosperity to himself and to the Black Hills. But as the twentieth century arrived, another opportunity presented itself. In 1901, President William McKinley appointed Bullock superintendent of the Black Hills Forest Reserve. Accepting the challenge, Bullock set out to connect the goals of the federal government with the desires of the local residents.

President Grover Cleveland had created the Black Hills Forest Reserve with an executive order in 1897. This order closed federal lands to logging, homesteading, and grazing, and it outraged area citizens, who formed committees, with Sol Star heading the Deadwood group, demanding a reversal of the proclamation. South Dakota's senator Richard F. Pettigrew responded with the Pettigrew Amendment to the Sundry Civil Act, also known as the Forest Management Act of 1897. While his legislation did not overturn the president's order, it did delay the mandate until March 1898. Pettigrew's action also established the first federal guidelines for managing a federal forest reserve. Some of the details still needed to be worked out, but when the Black Hills became a reserve in 1898, these regulations allowed for public use. Yet, Black Hills residents remained indignant, and it fell to the first forest supervisor, H. G. Hamaker, and the government's forest specialist, Gifford Pinchot, to make them understand and accept the forest's new status.[1]

Pinchot and Hamaker had nearly impossible jobs. In October and November of 1897, while the forest reserve designation was on hold, Pinchot came to the Black Hills to convince anyone who would listen, including Homestake Mine superintendent Thomas Grier, that federal control would bring benefits. Pinchot saw the Black Hills as a special case. Its timber was in greater demand than in any other reserve, and local residents mistakenly believed that the resource was inexhaustible. Pinchot hoped to use this area for experimentation, a place he could test federal policies. Once the forest became a reserve, Pinchot continued working with Grier to develop Timber Case No. 1, which made Homestake the first company in the country to purchase trees on a federal reserve and cut them under government supervision. [2]

A loyal Republican, Hamaker had gotten his job as a political favor when politicians in Indiana convinced McKinley to appoint him. Despite having no knowledge of the Black Hills or of forestry, Hamaker seemingly fulfilled his assignment. He hired rangers to check for fires and illegal logging, and he publicized the laws and regulations. Yet, little went right for the supervisor. Sawmill operators complained that tight regulations forced them out of business, while Pinchot lamented that Hamaker granted too many cutting permits to settlers and miners. In fact, Pinchot disliked Hamaker and treated him accordingly. Faced with so many protests and caught in a no-win situation, Hamaker left the job in 1901. [3]

Black Hills residents and timber users saw Hamaker's departure as their opportunity to gain control of the forest. They wanted a local man appointed to help alleviate their frustrations over the forest-reserve designation. The state's congressional delegation agreed, and the combined forces presented Bullock's name to President McKinley. To win McKinley over, they highlighted Bullock's background, which seemingly fit the position, including the fact that he was a "life long republican."[4] The Indiana delegation, however, insisted that the job was theirs to fill, as part of their continuing patronage. At this point, Vice-president Roosevelt intervened. He endorsed the idea that a Black Hills man should have the job, and McKinley appointed Bullock.[5] Soon after, Roosevelt sent Bullock a letter stating how pleased he was "to have a man of your type to execute the forest laws, for I know you will see to it that they are enforced absolutely without regard to anything but the law."[6]

While the people who supported Bullock expected more local control, Bullock himself realized that just appointing a Black Hills person would not guarantee success. He needed to make changes. When Hamaker was supervisor, he reported to the Department of Interior's regional superintendent in Sheridan, Wyoming. Besides the Black Hills reserve, this person also oversaw the Yellowstone, Big Horn, and Teton reserves. Bullock disliked having a middleman, and he convinced the secretary of the interior to detach the Black Hills from the Sheridan office and make it a separate reserve. Bullock then reported directly to the Washington office.[7] This move made him the first independent superintendent of the Black Hills Forest Reserve, and as Deadwood's *Pioneer-Times* reported, it would "increase the labors and responsibilities of the supervisor, but will expedite the business of the reserve and eliminate some of the red tape."[8]

Bullock also eliminated other impediments to his administration. Soon after taking his position, he claimed that Washington was sending "a lot of dudes out here as Forest Rangers." Bullock wanted western men, "who could sleep out in the open with or without a blanket, put out a fire, and catch a horse thief."[9] In February 1902, Bullock went to Washington to meet his superiors at the Department of Interior, to visit with his congressmen, and to spend time with Roosevelt, who had become president following McKinley's assassination in September 1901. After these meetings, including some informal sessions with Roosevelt, Bullock got the authority "to appoint his own assistants and to regulate affairs on the reserve as he deems to the best interests of the government."[10] In other words, Bullock got the power he wanted.

As Bullock studied the forest, he quickly recognized the heavy demand placed upon its resources. His office issued more grazing permits and authorized more timber sales than any other reserve, and he knew that for the good of the region, these and other uses needed to be closely monitored. To make his case, he developed a management rationale, couched in economic terms. "The permanent industries of the Black Hills," he wrote in 1904, "are wholly dependent upon timber and water; destroy one and these industries will disappear, while if both are destroyed, the 'richest 100 miles square' will become a desert."[11] Bullock established a forest office in Deadwood, from which he managed fifteen to twenty rangers. He selected these men for their practical skills, their ability to saddle, pack, and ride long days, and not for their forestry knowledge. Their tasks mainly involved watching for forest fires, preventing illegal timber harvests, and enforcing state and federal laws.[12] Bullock made it clear that his men were to enforce state game laws, which included stopping people from "killing fish by the use of dynamite."[13]

Bullock's forest management ideas coincided with Gifford Pinchot's multiple-use philosophy. Ever since his support of the Yellowstone National Park measure in the Montana legislature, Bullock had operated on the principle that land should be put to its optimum use, much as Pinchot did, and the new supervisor now applied that mentality to the reserve. Consequently, when Pinchot visited the Black Hills, the two men got along well. Superintendent Bullock also managed timber sales more successfully than his predecessor had, and he improved the quality of grazing lands in the Hills, which had been badly abused. He angered some farmers when he limited the size of herds allowed on the reserve, but he won back their support when he removed a grazing fee that had been imposed by the national office. As he explained to Pinchot, these people had been a great asset in fighting forest fires, and the tax was not just.[14]

Hand-in-hand with grazing, and perhaps causing more concern for Bullock, was the issue of forest homesteads. Prior to the forest's designation as a reserve, a settler could claim a homestead almost anywhere within the Black Hills. The new status ended all homesteading, causing many problems. Some legitimate homesteaders, who had settled before the closure date, had neglected to do their paperwork and were threatened with losing their farms. Another group of people ignored the reserve status and continued to claim land, while others just protested, saying that the Black Hills contained much agricultural land that should be open for settlement. The affected farmers formed protest groups, and Bullock, who had always placed a high value on agriculture, attended their meetings and promised compromises. At the same time, Bullock had little time for speculators and dishonest claimants. Nevertheless, he asked the South Dakota congressional delegation to pass legislation that would allow more farms on reserve land. And while the claimants waited for action, Bullock permitted them to maintain their holdings, as long as they seemed reasonable. Legislation came in 1906, after Bullock had left the forest supervisor's job, when Congress passed the Forest Homestead Act that allowed homesteaders to claim agricultural lands within the reserve.[15]

During his tenure as superintendent, Bullock's greatest problem was not a human one. An infestation of pine-bark beetles had begun about 1895, and over the next fourteen years, the insects killed at least one-third of the forest's trees. The years 1903 to 1905 were the epidemic's worst, when it fell to Bullock to fight the bug. Since he knew little about insects, Bullock relied on Pinchot for advice. One of their strategies called for the timber industry to harvest only infected trees, the idea being that quick removal would stop the insects' spread. People in the lumber business protested. They saw the diseased wood as inferior, but Bullock made it more attractive by simplifying the administrative procedures. Companies, such as McLaughlin Tie & Timber of Spearfish, harvested millions of board feet of dead and dying trees, cutting most into railroad ties.[16]

As the beetles continued their destruction, Bullock came up with other methods to stop their advance. In one instance, he tried to restore the woodpecker population. Woodpeckers ate beetles, but their numbers had declined because squirrels were destroying woodpecker eggs. He offered a bounty to eliminate squirrels: a box of cartridges for every three squirrel tails brought in. Soon he had over a thousand tails.[17] Experts in the forestry department denied that killing squirrels had any affect, but a ten-year-old Rochford boy told Bullock that he had seen a squirrel taking a woodpecker egg. "Supervisor Bullock stated that he would sooner accept this observation of the boy than all the learning of the scientists who deny that the squirrel ate woodpecker's eggs," the Deadwood newspaper reported.[18] Nothing, however, stopped the course of the beetles.

Because of excessive harvesting, fires, and beetle kill, the Black Hills had a sparse timber cover in the early twentieth century, with some areas completely denuded. Bullock and the forest service responded with a program of reforestation. In the winter of 1901–1902, the supervisor paid young people to harvest seeds from pine cones in order to broadcast them in burned areas. Reforestation became an ongoing program, and these efforts brought results.[19] Newspaperman Freeman Knowles commented in 1905 that the Hills had a large growth of timber where ten years before "the ground was as bare as the streets of a city."[20]

Bullock's energy and competence earned him more responsibilities. When the president created three small forest reserves—Slim Buttes, Cave Hills, and Short Pine Hills—in northwestern South Dakota, Bullock added them to his watch. Then in 1902, Roosevelt appointed him custodian of Wind Cave. Private entrepreneurs had opened the cave as a tourist attraction in the late nineteenth century, but conflicting claims brought litigation that resulted in the federal government withdrawing the cave site from private control. As Congress debated possible national park status for the cave, residents of the area wanted it reopened for tourists. Bullock's new position allowed him to name a supervisor, who would then employ guides. When Congress created Wind Cave National Park in 1903, Bullock retained his custodian status, becoming something of a middleman. While federal employees ran the attraction, Bullock made suggestions to them and to Washington about its operation. Among other things, he recommended that the regulations covering Yellowstone and Yosemite be applied to this park, and he investigated the possibility of introducing buffalo. He also blocked homesteaders from claiming more land in the surrounding forest, maintaining the integrity of the area.[21]

The Black Hills region saw three other major conservation projects in the early twentieth century: the creation of national monuments at Devils Tower and Jewel Cave and the construction of a dam and irrigation ditches at Belle Fourche. Some historians associate Bullock with each of these events, which seems possible. Bullock certainly had been to Devils Tower and undoubtedly appreciated its aesthetic value, much as he understood the natural beauty of Yellowstone Park. Similarly, he must have visited Jewel Cave and probably viewed it in the same light as Wind Cave. And since Roosevelt used a presidential proclamation to establish both monuments, it seems plausible that the two men discussed their importance. But there is no immediate evidence that connects Bullock to either decision.[22]

It is even more likely that Bullock had his hand in the Belle Fourche Irrigation Project. Bullock had a strong interest in water. When he published his rationale for forest management in 1904, he listed water and timber as the most important resources, and his statements paralleled those of Pinchot and Roosevelt. These men stressed water and forest conservation equally. As Roosevelt stated in his autobiography, "The Forest and water problems are perhaps the most vital internal problems of the United States."[23] Roosevelt consequently supported the Reclamation Act of 1902, which allowed the federal government to build dams and irrigation projects in sixteen western states and territories, including South Dakota. One year after the act's passage, Secretary of the Interior Ethan Hitchcock authorized the nation's first federally funded irrigation projects, but none were in South Dakota. He approved the Belle Fourche project in 1904.[24]

With Bullock's connections, it seems natural that the state's first major water project would be built on the Belle Fourche River, near the town of Belle Fourche. He knew the president, and while Roosevelt did not select the project locations, he certainly could have influenced the process. Further, Roosevelt understood the country in northwestern South Dakota, and it fit his criteria for reclamation. He intended the act to replace the herds of cattle and sheep of absentee owners with "actual homemakers, who have settled on the land with their families."[25] Bullock probably wanted the same thing, but of course, he would also benefit from increased land values. If Roosevelt did not weigh in on the selection, Bullock, as forest supervisor, could certainly have discussed reclamation sites with his boss, secretary Hitchcock. Like the monuments, however, no direct evidence links Bullock to this federal action.

While Bullock's political connections may have helped, most historical accounts credit local resident Peter P. Vallery with stimulating interest in the Belle Fourche project. In early 1903, he sent letters to South Dakota congressman Eben W. Martin and to the Department of the Interior asking them to consider the Belle Fourche River as an irrigation district. Two hundred Butte County residents followed up his request with a petition, calling on the government to build a reservoir. Bullock undoubtedly supported these initiatives and may have worked behind the scenes, convincing people to sign on. The superintendent had a long history with irrigation. When he and Star bought land for the S & B Ranch, they also acquired the water rights and an adjacent irrigation ditch. When Bullock introduced alfalfa to the Black Hills, the diverted water made its planting possible. As prospects of a dam project developed, Bullock began promoting another new crop: sugar beets. With adequate water, the sugar business could bring a new round of prosperity, which would help him financially and fulfill his vision of optimal resource utilization. It took the Bureau of Reclamation ten years to finish the Belle Fourche project, and by its conclusion, Bullock had sold land to the irrigation authority. Then, in 1916, the Great Western Sugar Company of Denver purchased a large portion of his ranch for a factory site.[26]

By 1905, Bullock's efforts for conservation, especially his work on the forest reserve, had gained him increased recognition. Black Hills newspapers began to praise him for carrying out his duties with "energy and thoroughness."[27] One article claimed that he had succeeded "in preserving the forest growth which for years had suffered at the hands of unheeding destroyers" and that he had won "the active cooperation of many men who at first were either actively or covertly hostile to the movement for forest preservation."[28] Bullock's work also attracted national attention. In January of 1905, he traveled to Washington to speak to the American Forestry Congress on how the mining industry benefited from proper timber management.[29] As Bullock arrived home, the Deadwood newspaper called the meeting "one of the most notable gatherings of recent years in the national capital." When the reporter asked Bullock for his impressions, the supervisor replied: "It was a respectable looking lot of wood-choppers."[30]

Chief Forester Pinchot asked Bullock to return to Washington in December 1905 for a forest service conference. The Deadwood newspaper again waxed eloquent, proclaiming, "Captain Bullock is recognized as one of the ablest and leading supervisors in the country." He had originated "many of the most practical suggestions that the department of forest reserve has adopted."[31] Bullock went to the meeting with two purposes: to discuss reseeding burned spots by scattering seed on snow and to help prepare a new forest-service rule book, or "usebook." But while in the East, Bullock learned that President Roosevelt had sent his name to the United States Senate for confirmation as United States marshal for the state of South Dakota. When the Senate approved his nomination, Bullock made a quick trip to the White House to thank his friend.[32]

As Bullock returned home in late December, most Black Hills residents celebrated. Deadwood's Hook and Ladder Company held a rousing reception, with dignitaries praising Bullock for his achievements as forest supervisor and expressing their confidence in the new marshal. "It was perhaps the proudest moment in my life when I received the appointment of the president," Bullock told the crowd, "but let me assure you that tonight is the happiest moment of my life."[33] Area newspapers added to the accolades, but with some ambivalence. The *Queen City Mail* of Spearfish regretted the loss of "one of the most popular men" in the forest service,[34] and the *Deadwood Pioneer-Times* reported that Bullock was one of the "best posted and most efficient men not even excepting the chief of the division of Forestry." The *Deadwood* article went on to state, "The captain will make as good a marshal as there is in the service,—and yet he is needed in the Forestry service where men of ability and sound business judgment are none too plentiful."[35]

Bullock's four-and-a-half-year tenure as superintendent of the reserve established the precedents that would allow the Black Hills forest to flourish. He worked with Gifford Pinchot, learning forestry techniques and developing his own policies. As Bullock gained more control, he brought more efficiency, while eliminating the stigma of federal power. Some people still hated the rules and complained about lost business, especially at the sawmills, but Bullock managed to dissipate much of the anger. He had been the key transitional figure in the administration of the Black Hills National Forest.[36]

The former superintendent moved on with little apparent regret, reveling in his new appointment as federal marshal. From his earliest days in Montana, he had always seen himself as a lawman. When he was sworn in on 1 February 1906, he was fifty-eight years old, and this position would allow him to wind down his career doing what he loved. Bullock's initial appointment lasted for four years. In 1909, President William H. Taft reappointed him, allowing Bullock to serve for a total of eight years. One correspondent observed, when Bullock became marshal, he obtained a "fat job," and the record seems to support that premise.[37] The position required that the marshal work out of Sioux Falls, but Bullock stayed in Deadwood. At his age, he was not about to move. His six deputies handled the day-to-day business, and he supervised them from his hometown. Two ran the Sioux Falls office, and four were stationed around the state.[38]

Bullock and his men had a number of responsibilities. They supported and managed the federal courts, which meant serving subpoenas and warrants, paying court expenses, which included fees for jurors and witnesses, and making sure that people came to court on time. Bullock also had to respond to federal crimes. He reported pursuing embezzlers and bootleggers and handling land fraud cases, a definite contrast to Bullock's relationship to the land laws in the 1870s and 1880s. Bullock and his deputies also had responsibility for federal crimes on the Indian reservations.[39] Here they dealt with horse thieves, whiskey traders, and, as Bullock commented, everything from "larceny to murder."[40] Given their heavy work loads, Bullock advocated that his men deserved more pay. In 1907, he wrote to the nation's attorney general, explaining that there were about twenty-five thousand American Indians in his district, and with the number of crimes, his deputies deserved extra money. He even invoked a little Roosevelt rhetoric, telling the attorney general that his deputies "were not getting a square deal in the matter of salaries."[41]

Bullock's job as marshal gave him plenty of time to travel, and he used some of it to visit Roosevelt. In late 1907, the president invited Bullock and his wife to stay at the White House. According to one observer, Roosevelt would call him to Washington because the marshal brought a "message of the plains, . . . the spirit of the great out-of-doors, and thus serve[d] his chief in this simple but most effective way."[42] Bullock went to the nation's capital again in early 1909, this time to attend Roosevelt's farewell party. Members of the "tennis cabinet" gathered at the White House to give him a send-off, and they invited a few of the president's friends, including Bullock, making them "honorary members" of the group. The thirty-one attendees gave Roosevelt a bronze cougar as a going-away gift, and it fell to Bullock to say a few words and unveil the trophy. As he occasionally admitted, however, Bullock was "a poor hand at saying good-by," and this event rendered him speechless.[43] When his time came, all he could do was push away the flowers hiding the gift, leaving another guest to give the address. Yet, the president rejoiced at Bullock's emotional display of friendship, placing him at his side in the photograph taken on the occasion.[44]

After leaving the presidency, Roosevelt went overseas, first to Africa and then to Europe. As he left Africa, he wired Bullock to join him in London. As Roosevelt explained in his autobiography, "by that time I felt that I just had to meet my own people, who spoke my neighborhood dialect."[45] A few years later, he commented to Estelline Bennett that he called for Bullock because "I wanted those Britishers to see my ideal typical American."[46] But Bullock claimed that Roosevelt needed him to "help him laugh," and the marshal did all he could to make that happen. As the two men strolled along the Thames River, Bullock stopped "a particularly haughty-looking Englishman" and asked him the name of this "creek." Bullock got the indignant response he wanted, causing Roosevelt to chuckle for a day. On another occasion, Bullock was queried why Roosevelt did not seem to care for kings. Bullock mused that the former president "preferred aces." And when he was questioned about how long he had known Roosevelt, Bullock replied, "From the tail of a chuck wagon (in the old round-up days) to the Court of St. James."[47]

Once he returned home, Bullock continued to support Roosevelt in any way he could. When Roosevelt decided to enter the presidential election of 1912, Bullock served as a political advisor and helped his campaign in South Dakota. Although Roosevelt lost the election, Bullock never lost faith in his friend's political savvy.[48] When Roosevelt supported Republican nominee Charles Evans Hughes in 1916, so did Bullock, but he was unconvinced about the wisdom of the Republican choice. In a letter to Kermit Roosevelt, Bullock wrote, "Hughes will owe his election wholly to the efforts of the Colonel [Roosevelt]."[49]

In 1914, Bullock left the marshal's office at the age of sixty-seven. He could have relaxed and reflected on a full life; instead, he remained active. When his wife Martha became president of the Deadwood Franchise League, for example, Bullock publicly supported woman's suffrage. He also maintained connections with a number of Belle Fourche businesses, such as the Belle Fourche Land and Cattle Company, but in late 1916, he closed most of these ventures when he sold much of his land to the Great Western Sugar Company.[50] He told Kermit Roosevelt that he made enough from the sale "to enable me to 'shoot ducks in Florida' for the balance of my days should I elect to do so, which I assuredly will not."[51]

Bullock could not retire, especially with Theodore Roosevelt as a friend. When war loomed with Mexico, Roosevelt talked of organizing a volunteer corps, much as he had done during the Spanish-American War, but nothing happened. With the entry of the United States into World War I, Roosevelt again moved to form volunteer units, asking Captain Bullock to form a troop. Bullock immediately went to work, and he later claimed to have enlisted twelve hundred men, which included four hundred Black Hills miners, four hundred railroad men, and four hundred cowboys from South Dakota, Montana, and Wyoming. But before organization could be perfected, President Wilson rejected the volunteer troops.[52]

Roosevelt and his followers were devastated. Forty of his prospective officers, including Bullock, were in New York to discuss the units when they learned about Wilson's decision. As they gathered at Sagamore Hill, Roosevelt read them a prepared statement explaining the situation. Bullock returned home in disgust, berating Wilson for his shortsightedness, but he still threw himself into the war effort. He chaired Lawrence County's Red Cross fund and its Exemption Board.[53] As he told Kermit, "We shall shew [sic] the democrats that we are thorobreds and will do our bit even if we are compelled to remain at home with the democrats." He went on, "I did want to ride a spotted cayuse into Berlin, it don't look now as I would."[54]

Bullock, however, could do little more for the war effort. He became ill in 1917 with what he described as the "grippe which ended in a stomach trouble." His stomach problems proved to be intestinal cancer, and he went to California for surgery. "Folks came to California after the remains," Bullock wrote to Kermit, "but when they arrived they found the remains sitting up and cussing the huns."[55] He spent the winter on the West Coast, and once he returned home in 1918, he regained some of his vigor. Then the news arrived of Theodore Roosevelt's death in January 1919. As Kermit Roosevelt said, "My father's death was a fearful blow to the old Captain."[56] With his remaining strength, Bullock convinced the Society of Black Hills Pioneers to commemorate his hero and friend. He had previously persuaded the organization to make Roosevelt the first honorary member, and the group now agreed to build a monument.[57]

While the monument was technically a Society of Black Hills Pioneer's project, Bullock himself picked the location, supervised the construction, and organized the dedication. Some people in Deadwood argued that it should be placed in town where visitors could easily see it. Bullock rejected that notion. He wanted a spot that reflected Roosevelt's West, with panoramic views of both the plains and the mountains. Further, he wanted it where people could touch the "wild outdoors which Theodore Roosevelt loved." Bullock envisioned it as "a national shrine" that would inspire visitors "to dream some of the dreams that Roosevelt dreamed."[58]

Bullock found his desired locale three miles north of Deadwood on Sheep Mountain. Getting the peak's name changed to Mount Roosevelt, Bullock had a thirty-five foot tower erected on its summit. Constructed out of local rock and cement, the tower acquired a rough texture, a look Bullock selected to reflect the character of the country. Yet, the structure itself looked much like the turret of a small castle. It was completed in a matter of months, and Bullock set the dedication of the monument for 4 July, sending invitations far and wide. Over a thousand people made the trek to Mount Roosevelt. Governor Peter Norbeck presided over the ceremonies. Roosevelt's close friend and former Rough Rider, Major General Leonard Wood, gave the keynote address, and Bullock watched with great satisfaction.[59]

Bullock, however, wore himself out, and as the summer of 1919 wound down, his health took a turn for the worse. His intestinal cancer returned and on 23 September 1919, at the age of seventy-three, Seth Bullock died in his home at 28 Van Buren Street in Deadwood. Just before he passed away, he had been negotiating to buy land at White Rocks. This property sat above Deadwood and provided a sweeping vista of the town, the Black Hills, and Mount Roosevelt. Bullock envisioned the Society of Black Hills Pioneers establishing a park on the land. Instead, he asked to be buried there. On 26 September, hundreds of people paid their last respects at the Bullock home and then followed the hearse up to the plot just below White Rocks. From this perch, Bullock could watch over the things that mattered most: Deadwood, the Black Hills, and Mount Roosevelt.[60]

Bullock's headstone carries a one-word epitaph: "Pioneer." To Bullock, a pioneer worked for progress, and through each stage of his life, he did just that. Nothing could better describe or summarize his life. From sheriff to forest supervisor to United States marshal, no matter the task, this pioneer lawman tried to advance the region and the country.

Notes

INTRODUCTION

1. Quoted in Travers D. Carman, "Captain Seth Bullock—A Black Hills Pioneer," *Outlook* 123 (29 Oct. 1919): 235.

2. William A. Remer, Diary, 15 Oct. 1896, and George E. Hair to Bob Crow, 24 Nov. 1926, Box 139, both in Adams Museum & House Archives, Deadwood, S.Dak.; Elting E. Morison, ed., *The Letters of Theodore Roosevelt*, 8 vols. (Cambridge, Mass.: Harvard University Press, 1951–1954), 3:560.

3. Kenneth C. Kellar, *Seth Bullock: Frontier Marshal* (Aberdeen, S.Dak.: North Plains Press, 1972); [Seth Bullock], *Seth Bullock's The Founding of a County: A Historical Sketch of Lawrence County, South Dakota, from His Records of 1876*, comp. P. H. Kellar (Deadwood, S.Dak.: By the Compiler, 1986); Clifford P. Westermeier, *Who Rush to Glory: The Cowboy Volunteers of 1898* (Caldwell, Idaho: Caxton Printers, 1958); Otto L. Sues, *Grigsby's Cowboys: Third United States Volunteer Cavalry, Spanish-American War* (Salem, S.Dak.: By the Author, 1900); Kermit Roosevelt, *The Happy Hunting-Grounds* (New York: Charles Scribner's Sons, 1920); Theodore Roosevelt, *An Autobiography* (New York: Macmillan Co., 1913); Morison, *Letters of Theodore Roosevelt*, vols. 1–3.

CHAPTER 1: FROM MONTANA TO DEADWOOD

1. Kenneth C. Kellar, *Seth Bullock: Frontier Marshal* (Aberdeen, S.Dak.: North Plains Press, 1972), pp. 9–19; *Helena Daily Independent*, 4, 8 July 1876.

2. *Helena Daily Independent*, 8 July 1876; Bullock to Chas. Warren, 8 Sept. 1876, printed in *Butte Miner*, 3 Oct. 1876; Jesse Brown and A. M. Willard, *The Black Hills Trails: A History of the Struggles of the Pioneers in the Winning of the Black Hills*, ed. John T. Milek (Rapid City, S.Dak.: Rapid City Journal Co., 1924), pp. 424–25.

3. Annie D. Tallent, *The Black Hills; or, The Last Hunting Ground of the Dakotahs*, 2d ed. (Sioux Falls, S.Dak.: Brevet Press, 1974), pp. 184–86, 191; Bob Lee, ed., *Gold, Gals, Guns, Guts: A History of Deadwood, Lead, and Spearfish, 1874–1976* (1976; reprint ed., Pierre: South Dakota State Historical Society Press, 2004), pp. 25–26; Brown and Willard, *Black Hills Trails*, p. 80.

4. [Seth Bullock], Seth Bullock's The Founding of a County: A Historical Sketch of Lawrence County, South Dakota, from His Records of 1876, comp. P. H. Kellar (Deadwood, S.Dak.: By the Compiler, 1986), p. 30 (the same material appeared earlier in Seth Bullock, "An Account of Deadwood and the Northern Black Hills in 1876," ed. Harry H. Anderson, South Dakota Historical Collections 31 [1962]: 287–364); Tallent, Black Hills, pp. 186–87; Kellar, Seth Bullock, p. 44; Helena Daily Independent, 8 July 1876; Deadwood Daily Pioneer-Times, 11 Oct. 1917; Seth Bullock to Edmund Seymour, 13 Aug. 1918, Edmund Seymour Collection, American Heritage Center, University of Wyoming, Laramie, Wyo.

5. Irma H. Klock, All Roads Lead to Deadwood (Lead, S.Dak.: By the Author, 1979), pp. 146–47; Kellar, Seth Bullock, p. 44; Deadwood Daily Pioneer-Times, 11 Oct. 1917.

6. Different dates have been given for Bullock and Star's arrival in Deadwood. Bullock's grandson published the date of 1 August in Kellar, Seth Bullock, p. 44, and this date is widely repeated. Deadwood pioneer John S. McClintock reported it as 31 July in his Pioneer Days in the Black Hills: Accurate History and Facts Related by One of the Early Day Pioneers, ed. Edward L. Senn (1939; reprint ed., Norman: University of Oklahoma Press, 2000), p. 294. The Black Hills Daily Pioneer, 5 Aug. 1876, gives the date as 4 August. The date of 3 August comes from a letter Seth Bullock wrote to Charles Warren, dated 8 September 1876, which was published in the Butte Miner, 3 Oct. 1876. The letter was written just over a month after Bullock arrived and should be reliable.

7. Black Hills Pioneer, 30 Sept., 7 Oct. 1876; Brown and Willard, Black Hills Trails, pp. 463, 470; Watson Parker, Deadwood: The Golden Years (Lincoln: University of Nebraska Press, 1981), p. 32.

8. Bullock, Founding of a County, pp. 32–34; Harry ("Sam") Young, Hard Knocks: A Life Story of the Vanishing West (1915; reprint ed., Pierre: South Dakota State Historical Society Press, 2005), pp. 221–22.

9. Deadwood Daily Pioneer-Times, 11 Oct. 1917; U. S., Department of the Interior, Bureau of the Census, Ninth Census of the United States, 1870, Deer Lodge Co., Mont., in AncestryLibrary.com (subscription required); Laura Floyd, "Deadwood's Political Star," Deadwood Magazine (Nov. 2006): 15.

10. Kellar, Seth Bullock, pp. 7–8. The date of Bullock's birth has been variously reported. His grandson gives 1849, and the United States census reports over the decades indicate 1849, 1850, and 1851

as possibilities. His obituary in the *Deadwood Daily Pioneer-Times*, 24 Sept. 1919, lists 1847. Also, Canada, *Census of Canada East, Canada West, New Brunswick, and Nova Scotia, 1851*, Canada West, Essex Co., Sandwich, in *AncestryLibrary.com*, indicates Bullock's birth as 1847.

11. Kellar, *Seth Bullock*, p. 8; Stanley Bullock, "The Bullock Family," in *Pioneer Footprints*, 3d ed. (Belle Fourche, S.Dak.: Black Hills Half Century Club, 1973), p. 12; Kermit Roosevelt, *The Happy Hunting-Grounds* (New York: Charles Scribner's Sons, 1920), p. 167.

12. Estelline Bennett, *Old Deadwood Days* (1928; reprint ed., Lincoln: University of Nebraska Press, 1982), p. 54.

13. Kellar, *Seth Bullock*, pp. 38, 44–45; *Black Hills Daily Times*, 26 Oct. 1878; *Census of Canada* (1851), Canada West, Essex Co., Sandwich.

14. *Helena Daily Herald*, 3 July 1871; *Helena Daily Independent*, 6 July 1876; *Ninth Census* (1870), Helena, Lewis & Clark, Co., Mont.; David Miller, "Black Hills Entrepreneur: Seth Bullock," in *South Dakota Leaders: From Pierre Chouteau, Jr., to Oscar Howe*, ed. Herbert T. Hoover & Larry J. Zimmerman (Vermillion: University of South Dakota Press, 1989), p. 234; Kellar, *Seth Bullock*, p. 13.

15. Clark C. Spence, *Territorial Politics and Government in Montana, 1864–89* (Urbana: University of Illinois Press, 1975), pp. 19–22; *Helena Daily Herald*, 31 July 1867; Kellar, *Seth Bullock*, pp. 8, 11–12.

16. Michael P. Malone and Richard B. Roeder, *Montana: A History of Two Centuries* (Seattle: University of Washington Press, 1976), pp. 84–85; Spence, *Territorial Politics and Government in Montana*, pp. 80–81, 117, 119, 129–35; *Helena Daily Herald*, 8 Aug. 1871; Miller, "Black Hills Entrepreneur," pp. 234–35; Kellar, *Seth Bullock*, pp. 8, 10, 14.

17. Miller, "Black Hills Entrepreneur," p. 235. *See also* John Hafnor, *Black Hills Believables: Items Panned from the Golden Past of Paha Sapa* (Billings, Mont.: Falcon Press Publishing Co., 1983), p. 44, and Kellar, *Seth Bullock*, p. 22.

18. Aubrey L. Haines, *The Yellowstone Story: A History of Our First National Park*, 2 vols. (Yellowstone National Park, Wyo.: Yellowstone Library & Museum Assoc., 1977), 1:109, 134–35, 166.

19. Quoted in Louis C. Cramton, *Early History of Yellowstone National Park and Its Relation to National Park Policies*, United States Department of the Interior (Washington, D.C.: Government Printing Office, 1932), p. 25.

20. Paul Schullery, *Searching for Yellowstone: Ecology and Wonder in the Last Wilderness* (Boston: Houghton Mifflin Co., 1997), pp. 60–61;

Cramton, *Early History of Yellowstone*, pp. 28–32; Haines, *The Yellowstone Story*, 1:164, 171.

21. Bullock Journal, Aug.-Sept. 1872, printed in Kellar, *Seth Bullock*, pp. 24, 26–28.

22. *Helena Daily Independent*, 25 June 1875.

23. Ibid., 2 Apr. 1874; *Helena Daily Herald*, 5 Aug. 1873.

24. Roosevelt, *Happy Hunting-Grounds*, p. 153; *Helena Daily Independent*, 14 Aug. 1875; *Helena Weekly Herald*, 19 Aug. 1875. *See also* Malone and Roeder, *Montana*, p. 64; Kellar, *Seth Bullock*, p. 10; Teresa Hamann, "Guide to the Execution Invitations Collection, 1875–1922," MSS 079, Maureen and Mike Mansfield Library, University of Montana, Missoula, in *Northwest Digital Archives*, http://nwda-db.wsulibs.wsu.edu, accessed 7/3/08.

25. *Helena Daily Independent*, 29 Oct. 1875. *See also Helena Weekly Herald*, 4 Nov. 1875.

26. Theodore Roosevelt to John Hay, 9 Aug. 1903, in *The Letters of Theodore Roosevelt*, ed. Elting E. Morison, 8 vols. (Cambridge: Harvard University Press, 1951–1954), 3:561

27. *Helena Daily Independent*, 21 June 1874. *See also* ibid., 24 Oct. 1875; Kellar, *Seth Bullock*, pp. 10–11; M. A. Leeson, *History of Montana, 1739–1885* (Chicago: Warner, Beers & Co., 1885), p. 673.

28. *Helena Daily Independent*, 21 June 1874; *Black Hills Daily Times*, 21 Apr. 1879; *Deadwood Daily Pioneer-Times*, 11 Oct. 1917, 24 Nov. 1918.

29. For more on the Panic of 1873, *see* M. John Lubetkin, *Jay Cooke's Gamble: The Northern Pacific Railroad, the Sioux, and the Panic of 1873* (Norman: University of Oklahoma Press, 2006).

30. [David A. Wolff], "Black Hills in Transition," in *A New South Dakota History*, ed. Harry F. Thompson (Sioux Falls, S.Dak.: Center for Western Studies 2005), pp. 293–96.

31. Malone and Roeder, *Montana*, p. 69; Ninth Census (1870), Deer Lodge Co., Lewis and Clark Co., Mont.

32. William A. Remer, Diary, 16 Aug. 1896, Adams Museum and House Archives, Deadwood, S.Dak.; *Black Hills Weekly and Whitewood Plaindealer*, 17 Mar. 1939; Kellar, *Seth Bullock*, pp. 42–43; Tenth Census (1880), Lawrence Co., D.T.

33. Brown and Willard, *Black Hills Trails*, pp. 463, 465; Kellar, *Seth Bullock*, p. 44.

34. Brown and Willard, *Black Hills Trails*, pp. 350, 470–71; *Black Hills Daily Times*, 19 May, 17 July 1877; Parker, *Deadwood*, pp. 59–61;

Lee, *Gold, Gals, Guns, Guts*, p. 22; *Black Hills Pioneer*, 29 July 1876.

35. Brown and Willard, *Black Hills Trails*, p. 469.

36. *Black Hills Pioneer*, 5 Aug. 1876.

37. Brown and Willard, *Black Hills Trails*, p. 381.

38. *Black Hills Daily Times*, 6 Mar. 1894.

39. Bullock to Warren, 8 Sept. 1876.

40. Bullock, *Founding of a County*, p. 58; Brown and Willard, *Black Hills Trails*, pp. 419–21.

41. Bullock to Warren, 8 Sept. 1876.

42. Bullock, *Founding of a County*, pp. 33, 37.

43. Glenn Chesney Quiett, *Pay Dirt: A Panorama of American Gold-Rushes* (New York: D. Appleton-Century Co., 1936), p. 248.

44. Leander P. Richardson, "A Trip to the Black Hills," *Scribner's Monthly* 13 (Apr. 1877): 756; Brown and Willard, *Black Hills Trails*, pp. 471–72.

45. Bullock, *Founding of a County*, pp. 30, 34; Kellar, *Seth Bullock*, p. 75.

46. Bullock, *Founding of a County*, p. 32. *See also Black Hills Pioneer*, 22 July 1876.

47. Parker, *Deadwood*, p. 42; Bullock, *Founding of a County*, pp. 63–64; *Black Hills Pioneer*, 7 Oct. 1876.

CHAPTER 2: ESTABLISHING THE LAW

1. Harry H. Anderson, "Deadwood, South Dakota: An Effort at Stability," *Montana, the Magazine of Western History* 20 (Jan. 1970): 43; *Black Hills Pioneer*, 19 Aug. 1876; [Seth Bullock], *Seth Bullock's The Founding of a County: A Historical Sketch of Lawrence County, South Dakota, from His Records of 1876*, comp. P. H. Kellar (Deadwood, S.Dak.: By the Compiler, 1986), p. 35.

2. Anderson, "Deadwood, South Dakota," pp. 43–44; *Black Hills Pioneer*, 19 Aug. 1876; Bullock, *Founding of a County*, p. 35; Bob Lee, ed., *Gold, Gals, Guns, Guts: A History of Deadwood, Lead, and Spearfish, 1874–1976* (1976; reprint ed., Pierre: South Dakota State Historical Society Press, 2004), p. 80.

3. Bullock, *Founding of a County*, pp. 35–36.

4. Ibid., pp. 38–39; John S. McClintock, *Pioneer Days in the Black Hills: Accurate History and Facts Related by One of the Early Day Pioneers*, ed. Edward L. Senn (1939; reprint ed., Norman: University of Oklahoma Press, 2000), pp. 121–23, 135–37; *Black Hills Pioneer*, 26 Aug.

1876; Jesse Brown and A. M. Willard, *The Black Hills Trails: A History of the Struggles of the Pioneers in the Winning of the Black Hills*, ed. John T. Milek (Rapid City, S.Dak.: Rapid City Journal Co., 1924), p. 483.

5. Bullock, *Founding of a County*, pp. 39, 42–43; *Black Hills Daily Times*, 4 Mar. 1883.

6. Bullock, *Founding of a County*, p. 39; *Black Hills Daily Times*, 25 Sept. 1883. Different accounts exist of this story. Another one can be found in McClintock, *Pioneer Days*, pp. 122–23. The *Black Hills Daily Times* article called the man "Texas Bill," not "Jack," and the perpetrator may have been selling pieces of skin instead of hair.

7. Bullock, *Founding of a County*, p. 39.

8. Ibid., pp. 44–45. *See also Black Hills Pioneer*, 26 Aug. 1876; *Black Hills Daily Times*, 4 Mar. 1880; James D. McLaird, Introduction to Harry ("Sam") Young's *Hard Knocks: A Life Story of the Vanishing West* (Pierre: South Dakota State Historical Society Press, 2005), pp. xi–xii. A slightly different account, with different names, exists in Robert J. Casey, *The Black Hills and Their Incredible Characters* (Indianapolis: Bobbs-Merrill Co., 1949), p. 151.

9. *Black Hills Pioneer*, 16 Sept. 1876.

10. Bullock, *Founding of a County*, p. 49; Lee, *Gold, Gals, Guns, Guts*, p. 81.

11. Bullock, *Founding of a County*, pp. 49–52; *Black Hills Pioneer*, 16 Sept., 28 Oct. 1876.

12. Kenneth C. Kellar, *Seth Bullock: Frontier Marshal* (Aberdeen, S.Dak.: North Plains Press, 1972), pp. 70, 102; Bullock, *Founding of a County*, pp. 70–71; *Black Hills Pioneer*, 21 Oct. 1876; *Deadwood Pioneer-Times*, 23 May 1952.

13. George W. Kingsbury, *History of Dakota Territory*, and George Martin Smith, *South Dakota: Its History and Its People*, 5 vols. (Chicago: S. J. Clarke Publishing Co., 1915), 1:976–78; Herbert S. Schell, *History of South Dakota*, 4th ed., rev. John E. Miller (Pierre: South Dakota State Historical Society Press, 2004), pp. 194–95; Lee, *Gold, Gals, Guns, Guts*, p. 83.

14. Kingsbury, *History of Dakota Territory*, 1:977–79; Kellar, *Seth Bullock*, p. 103; A. R. Z. Dawson to Governor Pennington, 17 Feb. 1877, and A. W. Adams to Governor Pennington, 21 Feb. 1877, both in John Pennington Papers, North Dakota State Archives and Library, Bismarck, N.Dak.

15. McClintock, *Pioneer Days*, p. 140.

16. *Black Hills Daily Times*, 13 Apr. 1877.

17. Ibid., 9, 12, 23 Apr. 1877; Howard Roberts Lamar, *Dakota Territory, 1861–1889: A Study of Frontier Politics* (New Haven, Conn.: Yale University Press, 1956), p. 161; Watson Parker, *Deadwood: The Golden Years* (Lincoln: University of Nebraska Press, 1981), p. 220; Bullock, *Founding of a County*, p. 72.

18. *Black Hills Daily Times*, 21 Apr. 1877, 31 Aug. 1887; *Black Hills Pioneer*, 24 Mar. 1877; Lee, *Gold, Gals, Guns, Guts*, pp. 85–86.

19. *Black Hills Daily Times*, 20 Aug., 7 Dec. 1877, 14 June 1878; *Black Hills Pioneer*, 5 May 1877; Kellar, *Seth Bullock*, p. 76.

20. *Black Hills Daily Times*, 5 Sept., 8 Oct. 1877; Kellar, *Seth Bullock*, pp. 78–80, 89–90.

21. *Black Hills Daily Times*, 14 May 1877.

22. The number of homicides are correlated from the lists of early Deadwood murders that appear in McClintock, *Pioneer Days*, pp. 270–74, and *Deadwood Weekly Pioneer-Times*, 7 Nov. 1901.

23. *Black Hills Pioneer*, 31 Mar. 1877.

24. *Black Hills Daily Times*, 24 Apr. 1877.

25. Quoted ibid., 27 Apr. 1877.

26. Ibid., 24, 26, 27 Apr. 1877. Brown and Willard, *Black Hills Trails*, p. 352, give an account of this event, but they cite the wrong year and spell the name of the man who died differently. McClintock, *Pioneer Days*, p. 272, also gives a different spelling for the man's name.

27. *Black Hills Daily Times*, 28, 30 Apr., 1 May, 19 June 1877.

28. Brown and Willard, *Black Hills Trails*, p. 352.

29. Ibid., pp. 358–59; *Black Hills Daily Times*, 4, 6 Oct. 1877.

30. *Black Hills Daily Times*, 5, 6 Sept. 1877; Joel Waterland, *The Spawn & the Mother Lode: The Story of the Placer, Conglomerate and Precambrian Mines of the Central City, Lead and Deadwood Area* ([Lead, S.Dak.]: By the Author, 1987), pp. 70–72.

31. *Black Hills Daily Times*, 5 Sept. 1877.

32. Brown and Willard, *Black Hills Trails*, p. 360; *Black Hills Daily Times*, 6, 13, 19 Sept. 1877; Waterland, *Spawn & the Mother Lode*, pp. 72–73.

33. Irma H. Klock, *All Roads Lead to Deadwood* (Lead, S.Dak.: By the Author, 1979), pp. 27–28.

34. Brown and Willard, *Black Hills Trails*, p. 247; *Black Hills Daily Times*, 13 Apr. 1877, 22 Jan. 1878.

35. Estelline Bennett, *Old Deadwood Days* (1928; reprint ed., Lincoln: University of Nebraska Press, 1982), p. 61; *Black Hills Daily Times*, 13 Apr. 1877, 22 Jan., 19 Feb., 20 Dec. 1878, 31 Mar. 1879.

36. Brown and Willard, *Black Hills Trails*, pp. 255–56; *Black Hills Daily Times*, 27 Aug. 1877.

37. *Black Hills Daily Times*, 20, 23, 24, 25 Oct. 1877; Brown and Willard, *Black Hills Trails*, pp. 259–60.

38. *Black Hills Daily Times*, 24 Oct. 1877.

39. Brown and Willard, *Black Hills Trails*, p. 112; *Black Hills Daily Times*, 23 July 1877.

40. Brown and Willard, *Black Hills Trails*, pp. 112–14; *Black Hills Daily Times*, 23, 24 July 1877.

41. *Black Hills Daily Times*, 26 July 1877.

42. Quoted ibid., 27 July 1877.

43. Ibid., 27, 28 July 1877.

44. Kingsbury, *History of Dakota Territory*, 1:978.

45. Larry D. Ball, "A Contractor's Cussedness: Politics, Labor, Law, and the Keets Mine Incident of 1877," *South Dakota History* 26 (Summer/Fall 1996): 97, 114.

46. Bennett, *Old Deadwood Days*, p. 52.

47. Kellar, *Seth Bullock*, pp. 97–98.

48. Ball, "Contractor's Cussedness," pp. 104–13; *Black Hills Daily Times*, 8, 9 Nov. 1877.

49. Ball, "Contractor's Cussedness," pp. 113–14, 118–20.

50. *Black Hills Daily Times*, 26 May, 11, 14, 19 June, 7 July, 28 Aug., 28 Sept., 8, 15, 26 Oct., 4 Dec. 1877.

51. Ibid., 3, 7 Aug. 1877.

CHAPTER 3: STRUGGLING FOR DIRECTION

1. *Black Hills Daily Times*, 18 Sept., 3, 26 Oct. 1877.

2. Ibid., 4 Oct. 1877.

3. Ibid., 12, 20, 22 Oct. 1877; Howard Roberts Lamar, *Dakota Territory, 1861–1889: A Study of Frontier Politics* (New Haven, Conn.: Yale University Press, 1956), pp. 163–64; George W. Kingsbury, *History of Dakota Territory*, and George Martin Smith, *South Dakota: Its History and Its People*, 5 vols. (Chicago: S. J. Clarke Publishing Co., 1915), 1:979.

4. *Black Hills Daily Times*, 19, 26, 30 Oct., 2, 5 Nov. 1877; Lamar, *Dakota Territory*, pp. 163–64.

5. *Black Hills Daily Times*, 2 Nov. 1877.

6. Ibid., 27 Oct. 1877.

7. Ibid., 26 May, 24 Oct., 2, 6, 8, 10 Nov. 1877, 21 Apr. 1881; Lamar, *Dakota Territory*, p. 164.

8. Jesse Brown and A. M. Willard, *The Black Hills Trails: A History of the Struggles of the Pioneers in the Winning of the Black Hills*, ed. John T. Milek (Rapid City, S.Dak.: Rapid City Journal Co., 1924), pp. 364–65; Lamar, *Dakota Territory*, p. 165; Bob Lee, ed., *Gold, Gals, Guns, Guts: A History of Deadwood, Lead, and Spearfish, 1874–1976* (1976; reprint ed., Pierre: South Dakota State Historical Society Press, 2004), pp. 85, 95–97.

9. *Black Hills Daily Times*, 7, 8 Nov., 27, 28 Dec. 1877, 3 Dec. 1879; Lee, *Gold, Gals, Guns, Guts*, pp. 85–86; Kingsbury, *History of Dakota Territory*, 1:980.

10. *Black Hills Daily Times*, 4 Dec. 1877; Lee, *Gold, Gals, Guns, Guts*, p. 75; John Hafnor, *Black Hills Believables: Items Panned from the Golden Past of Paha Sapa* (Billings, Mont.: Falcon Press Publishing Co., 1983), p. 44; Alan L. Clem and James Rumbolz, *Law Enforcement: The South Dakota Experience* (Sturgis: South Dakota Peace Officers' Assoc., 1982), p. 128; John S. McClintock, *Pioneer Days in the Black Hills: Accurate History and Facts Related by One of the Early Day Pioneers*, ed. Edward L. Senn (1939; reprint ed., Norman: University of Oklahoma Press, 2000), pp. 273–74; *Deadwood Weekly Pioneer-Times*, 7 Nov. 1901.

11. Estelline Bennett, *Old Deadwood Days* (1928; reprint ed., Lincoln: University of Nebraska Press, 1982), p. 53.

12. Louis S. Warren, *Buffalo Bill's America: William Cody and the Wild West Show* (New York: Alfred A. Knopf, 2005), pp. 225–27.

13. For more on the legendary status of Hickok and Calamity Jane, *see* James D. McLaird, *Wild Bill Hickok and Calamity Jane: Deadwood Legends*, South Dakota Biography Series, no. 2 (Pierre: South Dakota State Historical Society Press, 2008).

14. Frederick S. Calhoun, *The Lawmen: United States Marshals and Their Deputies, 1789–1989* (Washington, D.C.: Smithsonian Institution Press, 1989), pp. 3, 7, 150; *Black Hills Daily Times*, 10, 14, 30 Sept. 1877, 6 Apr., 5 July 1878; Kenneth C. Kellar, *Seth Bullock: Frontier Marshal* (Aberdeen, S.Dak.: North Plains Press, 1972), pp. 111–18.

15. Brown and Willard, *Black Hills Trails*, pp. 262–68; Irma H. Klock, *All Roads Lead to Deadwood* (Lead, S.Dak.: By the Author, 1979), pp. 33–34; *Black Hills Journal*, 5 Oct. 1878; *Black Hills Daily Times*, 28,

30 Sept. 1878, 2 Apr. 1880; *Deadwood Daily Pioneer-Times*, 3 May 1902.

16. Seth Bullock, "Early Day Bandits," in *Deadwood Daily Pioneer-Times*, 3 May 1902. Bullock's memoir of the robbery and chase appeared under the same title on the front page of each issue of the *Deadwood Daily Pioneer-Times* from 3 through 9 May 1902.

17. *Western Enterprise* (Deadwood), cited in *Black Hills Daily Times*, 3 Oct. 1878.

18. Bullock, "Early Day Bandits," 7, 8 May 1902.

19. *Black Hills Daily Times*, 13 Sept. 1877, 27 Apr. 1878; Jill Pontius, "Deadwood Volunteer Fire Department," in *Some History of Lawrence County* (Deadwood, S.Dak.: Lawrence County Historical Society, 1981), pp. 572–73.

20. *Black Hills Daily Times*, 27 Apr. 1878.

21. Ibid., 13 Apr., 18 May, 3, 7 June, 2, 3, 5 July 1878.

22. Ibid., 9, 11 July, 13, 20 Dec. 1878.

23. Ibid., 21 Oct., 13 Dec. 1878, 19 Apr., 10 May, 11 Sept. 1879; Pontius, "Deadwood Volunteer Fire Department," p. 573.

24. *Black Hills Daily Times*, 14 Sept. 1878.

25. *Yankton Press and Dakotian*, quoted in *Black Hills Daily Times*, 7 Sept. 1878.

26. *Black Hills Daily Times*, 4 Sept. 1878. *See also* 14 Sept.

27. Ibid., 4 Nov. 1878.

28. Ibid., 16 Oct. 1878. *See also* 23 Oct.

29. Ibid., 7 Nov. 1878.

30. Ibid., 23 Apr. 1879.

31. Ibid., 7 Nov. 1878.

32. Ibid., 10 July 1878, 24 Feb., 31 Mar., 29 Apr., 17 May, 1 June, 11, 12 July 1879; George P. Baldwin, ed., *The Black Hills Illustrated: A Terse Description of Conditions Past and Present of America's Greatest Mineral Belt* (Deadwood, S.Dak.: Black Hills Mining Men's Assoc., 1904), p. 57.

33. *Black Hills Daily Times*, 18 Mar., 19, 24 June, 12 July 1879, 5 Sept., 31 Oct. 1881.

34. Ibid., 3 Mar. 1877, 21 Jan. 1878, 13 July 1879; David Miller, "Black Hills Entrepreneur: Seth Bullock," in *South Dakota Leaders: From Pierre Chouteau, Jr., to Oscar Howe*, ed. Herbert T. Hoover & Larry J. Zimmerman (Vermillion: University of South Dakota Press, 1989), p. 238; Kellar, *Seth Bullock*, pp. 94, 111–12; Baldwin, *Black Hills Illustrated*, p. 61; W. G. Rice, "Deadwood's Influence on the Development of the

Black Hills," *Black Hills Engineer* 18 (Jan. 1930): 56. Like everyone else in the region, Bullock initially ignored the land laws, which was easy to do because the northern plains had yet to be surveyed. Eventually he either had employees file land claims for him, or he bought the land from homesteaders who had proved up with no intention to settle. Miller, "Black Hills Entrepreneur," p. 238; Lucy Lytton Peterson, "Seth Bullock—Key Factor in the Birth of Belle Fourche," in *A History of Butte County, South Dakota*, comp. Pat Engebretson, Kay Heck, & Helen Herrett (Dallas, Tex.: Curtis Media Corp., 1989), p. 24.

35. Watson Parker, *Deadwood: The Golden Years* (Lincoln: University of Nebraska Press, 1981), pp. 33–34, 99.

36. *Black Hills Daily Times*, 27, 30 Sept., 1 Oct., 4 Nov. 1879; Brown and Willard, *Black Hills Trails*, pp. 438–40.

37. *Black Hills Daily Times*, 27 Sept., 4 Nov. 1879.

38. Rodman Wilson Paul, *Mining Frontiers of the Far West, 1848–1880* (New York: Holt, Rinehart & Winston, 1963), pp. 177–78.

CHAPTER 4: BUILDING UPON THE ASHES

1. R[ichard] F. Pettigrew, "Pettigrew Visits the Black Hills," *The Sunshine State* 7 (Mar. 1926): 39–40.

2. *Black Hills Daily Times*, 30 Sept., 1, 2 Oct. 1879.

3. Ibid., 4 Nov. 1879.

4. Ibid., 2 Oct. 1879.

5. Ibid., 8 Oct., 4 Nov. 1879.

6. Ibid., 8 Oct. 1879, 11, 12 Feb. 1881; Bob Lee, ed., *Gold, Gals, Guns, Guts: A History of Deadwood, Lead, and Spearfish, 1874–1976* (1976; reprint ed., Pierre: South Dakota State Historical Society Press, 2004), pp. 144–45.

7. *Black Hills Daily Times*, 25 Mar., 3 June 1880.

8. Ibid., 26 Feb. 1879.

9. Watson Parker, *Deadwood: The Golden Years* (Lincoln: University of Nebraska Press, 1981), p. 228; U.S., Department of the Interior, Bureau of the Census, *Tenth Census of the United States,1880*, Lawrence Co., D.T.; *Black Hills Daily Times*, 20 Oct. 1880.

10. *Black Hills Daily Times*, 10 Sept. 1880. *See also* 30 Apr., 19 May, 9 July 1880.

11. Mark S. Wolfe, *Boots on Bricks: A Walking Tour of Historic Downtown Deadwood* (Deadwood, S.Dak.: Deadwood Historic Preservation Commission, 1996), p. 66.

12. *Black Hills Daily Times,* 10 Aug. 1880, 15 July, 24 Oct. 1881, 3 July, 19 Oct., 1 Nov. 1887; *Black Hills Weekly Times,* 23 Feb. 1884; *Sturgis Weekly Record,* 5 Nov. 1886.

13. *Black Hills Daily Times,* 28 Mar., 30 Sept. 1880; *Spearfish Register,* cited in *Black Hills Daily Times,* 16 July 1881; *Tenth Census* (1880), Lawrence Co., Pennington Co., D.T.

14. "John C. and Elizabeth (Ash) Eccles," in *Pioneer Footprints,* 3d ed. (Belle Fourche, S.Dak.: Black Hills Half Century Club, 1973), p. 113; *Black Hills Daily Times,* 16 Apr., 18 Aug. 1882, 16 June 1883, 18 Jan., 13 Aug., 23 Sept. 1884, 10 Sept. 1885, 1 Jan. 1888.

15. "Star & Bullock," Lawrence County Property Tax Records, 1881, Leland D. Case Library for Western Historical Studies, Black Hills State University, Spearfish, S.Dak.; Lawrence County Property Records, Book 16, pgs. 226–27, Lawrence County Courthouse, Deadwood, S.Dak.; Land Patent Results List, Butte Co., S.Dak., Sec. no. 2, Township 8-N, Range 2-E, *Bureau of Land Management, Government Land Office Records,* www.glorecords.blm.gov, accessed 7/12/2007.

16. Joe Koller, "Minnesela Days," *South Dakota Historical Collections* 24 (1949): 37–38; Bob Lee and Dick Williams, *Last Grass Frontier: The South Dakota Stock Grower Heritage* (Sturgis, S.Dak.: Black Hills Publishers, 1964), pp. 75, 89, 97, 102; *Black Hills Daily Times,* 1 May 1881.

17. Koller, "Minnesela Days," pp. 17–23, 29–30, 80.

18. Ibid., pp. 13, 15, 24–26, 48.

19. Ibid., pp. 38, 60; Land Patent Results List, Butte Co., S.Dak., Sec. no. 10, Township 8-N, Range 2-E, www.glorecords.blm.gov, accessed 2/12/2007.

20. *Black Hills Daily Times,* 3 July 1887.

21. Seth Bullock to Charles C. Haas, 3 Dec. 1914, Alfalfa Controversy File (H84.14), South Dakota State Historical Society, Pierre, S.Dak.; Jesse Brown and A. M. Willard, *The Black Hills Trails: A History of the Struggles of the Pioneers in the Winning of the Black Hills,* ed. John T. Milek (Rapid City, S.Dak.: Rapid City Journal Co., 1924), pp. 505–6; Koller, "Minnesela Days," p. 13; *Black Hills Daily Times,* 5 Oct. 1880, 4 Aug. 1881, 14 Apr. 1885.

22. *Black Hills Daily Times,* 16 May 1886.

23. Ibid., 3 July 1887.

24. Ibid., 25 Dec. 1879.

25. Ibid., 1 Feb. 1881.

26. Ibid., 1, 17 Feb. 1881. For more on Benteen's tenure at the

fort, *see* Robert Lee, *Fort Meade & the Black Hills* (Lincoln: University of Nebraska Press, 1991), pp. 23, 64–65, 77.

27. *Black Hills Daily Times*, 1 May 1881.

28. Ibid., 19 Sept. 1881.1

29. Ibid., 19 Mar. 1884.

30. Ibid., 5, 21 June 1885, 11 Sept. 1886.

31. Ibid., 20 Jan., 27 June 1884, 22 May 1885, 26 Aug. 1886.

32. Ibid., 7, 13, 14, 28 Mar. 1884.

33. Lee and Williams, *Last Grass Frontier*, pp. 114–16; *Black Hills Daily Times*, 14 Mar., 6 Aug., 2 Nov. 1884.

34. *Black Hills Daily Times*, 25 Apr. 1884.

35. Ibid., 9 May 1885.

36. Koller, "Minnesela Days," pp. 50–51.

37. Ibid., p. 58; "Minnesela, DeMores, and the Start of Belle Fourche," in *Pioneer Footprints*, p. 75.

38. *Black Hills Daily Times*, 29 Aug. 1885, 3 July 1887.

39. David A. Wolff, "Pyritic Smelting at Deadwood: A Temporary Solution to Refractory Ores," *South Dakota History* 15 (Winter 1985): 312–15.

40. *Black Hills Daily Times*, 30 Jan. 1881.

41. Ibid., 8 Feb. 1881.

42. *The Black Hills of Dakota, 1881* (Deadwood, D.T.: Deadwood Board of Trade, 1881), p. 6.

43. *Black Hills Daily Times*, 17 Feb., 2 Mar. 1881.

44. Ibid., 6 Feb. 1881.

45. Ibid., 27 Apr., 28 May 1881.

46. Ibid., 24 Feb. 1881.

47. Ibid., 25 Feb. 1881.

48. Ibid., 24 Feb., 20 Apr. 1881.

49. Ibid., 16 Dec. 1881.

50. Ibid., 24 Feb., 20, 27 Apr. 1881, 20 Feb. 1882.

51. Estelline Bennett, *Old Deadwood Days* (1928; reprint ed., Lincoln: University of Nebraska Press, 1982), p. 62; John S. McClintock, *Pioneer Days in the Black Hills: Accurate History and Facts Related by One of the Early Day Pioneers*, ed. Edward L. Senn (1939; reprint ed., Norman: University of Oklahoma Press, 2000), p. 294; William A. Remer, Diary, 16 Nov. 1896, Adams Museum and House Archives, Deadwood, S.Dak.; *Black Hills Daily Times*, 1 Oct. 1882, 27 July, 22 Nov. 1883, 3, 10 June, 9 Oct. 1884; *Deadwood Daily Pioneer-Times*, 11

Oct. 1917; *Andrea's Historical Atlas of Dakota* (Chicago: A. T. Andreas, 1884), p. 124.

52. *Black Hills Daily Times*, 4 May, 27 July, 1, 13 Aug., 8 Nov. 1881.

53. Ibid., 6, 8, 11, 18, 20 Feb. 1882.

54. Ibid., 20 Oct. 1881; Wolff, "Pyritic Smelting at Deadwood," pp. 314–15; Mildred Fielder, *Silver is the Fortune* (Aberdeen, S.Dak.: North Plains Press, 1978), pp. 18–19.

55. *Black Hills Daily Times*, 2 Dec. 1881.

56. Ibid., 2 Nov. 1881, 12 Apr. 1883.

57. Ibid., 5 Dec. 1882.

58. Ibid., 18 Apr., 19, 20, 23 May 1883.

59. Ibid., 15 June, 14 July, 31 Oct. 1883.

CHAPTER 5: A FRENZY OF SPECULATION

1. *Black Hills Daily Times*, 12 Mar., 1 May 1880, 19 Feb. 1887.

2. R. E. Driscoll, *Seventy Years of Banking in the Black Hills* (Rapid City: Gate City Guide, 1948), p. 67.

3. Ibid., pp. 31, 67–68; *Black Hills Daily Times*, 2 Nov. 1881, 26 Oct. 1886, 17, 19 Feb. 1887; *Deadwood Daily Pioneer-Times*, 14 Dec. 1898.

4. *Black Hills Daily Times*, 18 Feb. 1887.

5. Ibid., 17, 18 Feb. 1887.

6. Ibid., 27 Mar., 19 Apr., 9 Aug., 13 Oct. 1887, 29 Apr., 9 May 1888; *Black Hills Weekly Times*, 16 June 1894.

7. *Black Hills Daily Times*, 6, 11, 15 Aug., 1, 2 Sept., 18 Nov. 1881, 7 June 1882, 21 Mar. 1886; Joel K. Waterland, The *Mines Around & Beyond: The History of the Deadwood, Two Bit, . . . and Tinton Mining Districts, Black Hills of South Dakota* (Lead, S.Dak.: By the Author, 1991), p. 226.

8. *Black Hills Daily Times*, 12 Apr., 1, 7 June, 14 Aug., 10 Nov. 1883, 23 July 1886.

9. Ibid., 9 Oct., 21, 22 Nov. 1884, 6 Feb., 1 Dec. 1885.

10. Ibid., 22 Nov. 1884.

11. Ibid., 11 Mar., 2, 3 June 1885, 2 Feb. 1886.

12. Ibid., 3 July, 1 Aug. 1885.

13. Ibid., 7, 14 July 1885, 13 Mar. 1886. For a description of stamp mills, smelters, and milling processes, *see* Richmond L. Clow, *Chasing the Glitter: Black Hills Milling, 1874–1959*, Historical Preservation Series, no. 2 (Pierre: South Dakota State Historical Society Press, 2002).

14. *Black Hills Daily Times*, 1 Aug., 28, 29 Nov., 1 Dec. 1885, 26 Jan. 1886.

15. Ibid., 10 Mar. 1886. *See also* 18 June.

16. Ibid., 6 May 1886.

17. Ibid., 4 Feb. 1886.

18. Ibid., 5 Feb., 9 May 1886.

19. Estelline Bennett, *Old Deadwood Days* (1928; reprint ed., Lincoln: University of Nebraska Press, 1982), p. 19; Watson Parker, *Deadwood: The Golden Years* (Lincoln: University of Nebraska Press, 1981), p. 149.

20. *Black Hills Daily Times*, 30 Apr. 1886.

21. Ibid., 3 Feb. 1886.

22. Ibid., 11 June 1886. *See also* 2 Feb.

23. Ibid., 6 Mar. 1886.

24. Ibid., 1 June 1886.

25. Ibid., 18 Jan., 22 May 1885, 21 Jan., 16 May, 27 June 1886.

26. Ibid., 3, 7, 9 Feb., 6 July 1886; *Deadwood Weekly Pioneer-Times*, 23 May 1901.

27. *Black Hills Daily Times*, 21 Feb. 1886.

28 Quoted ibid.,11 June 1886.

29. Ibid., 12, 18 June 1886, 13 Mar. 1887.

30. Ibid., 6, 16 May, 2, 17, 20, 22 July, 3 Oct., 21 Nov. 1886.

31. Ibid., 20 July 1886.

32. Ibid., 20, 21 July, 15 Oct., 11 Nov. 1886; Driscoll, *Seventy Years of Banking*, pp. 31, 68.

33. *Black Hills Daily Times*, 20 July 1886. *See also* 21 July, 1 Aug.

34. Ibid., 23 July 1886.

35. Ibid., 1 Sept. 1886.

36. Ibid., 2 Nov. 1886.

37. Ibid., 20 Jan., 6 Feb. 1887.

38. Ibid., 3, 6, 17, 19 Feb. 1887, 4 June 1890.

39. Ibid., 3, 6 Mar., 31 July 1887.

40. Ibid., 14 June 1887.

41. Ibid., 16 June 1887.

42. Ibid., 8 Oct. 1886, 26 Aug., 7 Sept. 1887.

43. Ibid., 9 Sept. 1887.

44. Ibid., 2, 6 Nov. 1887, 4 Jan., 25, 29 Feb., 3, 6 Mar. 1888.

45. Ibid., 6 Dec. 1887.

46. Ibid., 7 Mar. 1888.

47. Ibid., 6, 28 June 1888, 3 June 1891.

48. Ibid., 17, 25 Feb. 1887; Joe Koller, "Minnesela Days," *South Dakota Historical Collections* 24 (1949): 64.

49. *Black Hills Daily Times*, 5 Feb. 1887.

50. Ibid., 20 Sept. 1887.

51. Ibid., 30 Mar., 8 Dec. 1886, 7 Oct. 1893; "Star & Bullock," Lawrence County Property Tax Records, 1898, Leland D. Case Library for Western Historical Studies, Black Hills State University, Spearfish, S.Dak.

52. *Black Hills Daily Times*, 12 Apr. 1887; Bob Lee and Dick Williams, *Last Grass Frontier: The South Dakota Stock Grower Heritage* (Sturgis, S.Dak.: Black Hills Publishers, 1964), p. 161; Star and Bullock Hardware Co., "Articles of Incorporation," 27 Sept. 1886, Office of the Secretary of State, Domestic Articles of Incorporation Ledgers, 1878–1970, Box 11, 1886–1887, State Archives Collection, South Dakota State Historical Society, Pierre, S.Dak.

53. *Black Hills Daily Times*, 1 Jan. 1888.

54. Ibid., 13 Sept. 1887.

55. Ibid., 14 Aug. 1888.

56. Ibid., 3 Dec. 1887, 14 June, 9 Sept. 1888, 18 May 1890.

57. Ibid., 8 June 1887, 13 Mar., 27 May 1888, 1 Jan. 1891; David A. Wolff, "Pyritic Smelting at Deadwood: A Temporary Solution to Refractory Ores," *South Dakota History* 15 (Winter 1985): 318.

58. David A. Wolff, "No Matter How You Do It, Fraud is Fraud: Another Look at Black Hills Mining Scandals," *South Dakota History* 33 (Summer 2003): 107–11; Wolff, "Pyritic Smelting," pp. 321–23.

59. Quoted in *Black Hills Daily Times*, 4 June 1890.

60. Wolff, "Pyritic Smelting," pp. 323–25; *Black Hills Daily Times*, 13, 15 Dec. 1889.

61. *Black Hills Daily Times*, 15 Dec. 1889.

62. Wolff, "Pyritic Smelting," pp. 324–32.

63. *Black Hills Daily Times*, 3, 4 June, 8, 9, 10 July 1890, 3 June 1891.

64. Ibid., 4 June 1890. The figures in this paragraph come from Bullock's 1890 report. Other sources contain slightly different information. George P. Baldwin, ed., *The Black Hills Illustrated: A Terse Description of Conditions Past and Present of America's Greatest Mineral Belt* (Deadwood, S.Dak.: Black Hills Mining Men's Assoc., 1904), p. 45,

gives production figures for the company of $736,000 and dividends of $165,250. J. D. Irving, *Economic Resources of the Northern Black Hills*, United States Geological Survey, Professional Paper, no. 26 (Washington: Government Printing Office, 1904), p. 177, gives a production figure of $667,218.

CHAPTER 6: RECOVERY

1. *Black Hills Daily Times*, 1 Jan. 1888; George P. Baldwin, ed., *The Black Hills Illustrated: A Terse Description of Conditions Past and Present of America's Greatest Mineral Belt* (Deadwood, S.Dak.: Black Hills Mining Men's Assoc., 1904), p. 73.

2. *Black Hills Daily Times*, 10 Aug., 19 Sept. 1888, 15 May 1890; Mildred Fielder, *Railroads of the Black Hills* (New York: Bonanza Books, 1964), pp. 62, 70–71.

3. *Black Hills Daily Times*, 30 Dec. 1890, 29 Jan. 1891.

4. Ibid., 27 May 1890.

5. Ibid., 23 Feb. 1890.

6. Ibid., 13 Mar., 7 May 1890; Lawrence County Property Records, 1890, Lawrence County Courthouse, Deadwood, S.Dak.

7. *Black Hills Daily Times*, 5 Aug. 1890. *See also Deadwood Daily Pioneer*, 6 Aug. 1890.

8. Joe Koller, "Minnesela Days," *South Dakota Historical Collections* 24 (1949): 19–20, 48, 74–75, 98–99.

9. Ibid., pp. 99–100; R. E. Driscoll, *Seventy Years of Banking in the Black Hills* (Rapid City: Gate City Guide, 1948), pp. 40–42.

10. Quoted in Driscoll, *Seventy Years of Banking*, p. 42.

11. Stanley Bullock, "The Bullock Family," in *Pioneer Footprints*, 3d ed. (Belle Fourche, S.Dak.: Black Hills Half Century Club, 1964), p. 12; Shirley O'Leary, "Belle Fourche Historic Homes and Business District," in *A History of Butte County, South Dakota*, comp. Pat Engebretson, Kay Heck, & Helen Herrett (Dallas, Tex.: Curtis Media Corp., 1989), p. 34; Butte County Property Records, Reference Book 2, Butte County Courthouse, Belle Fourche, S.Dak.; Koller, "Minnesela Days," p. 106.

12. Koller, "Minnesela Days," pp. 95–106; Kenneth C. Kellar, *Seth Bullock: Frontier Marshal* (Aberdeen, S.Dak.: North Plains Press, 1972), p. 118; Joe Koller, "Minnesela-Belle Fourche Feud," in *History of Butte County*, p. 47.

13. Michael Edgar Varney, "The History of the Chicago and North

Western Railway's Black Hills Division" (M.A. thesis, University of Wyoming, 1963), pp. 59, 76–77; Driscoll, *Seventy Years of Banking*, p. 42; "Minnesela, DeMores, and the Start of Belle Fourche," in *Pioneer Footprints*, pp. 75–76.

14. "Belle Fourche, Bullock's Town," in *Pioneer Footprints*, pp. 125–26; George E. Hair to Bob Crow, 24 Nov. 1926, Box 139, Adams Museum & House Archives, Deadwood, S.Dak.

15. "Belle Fourche, Bullock's Town," p. 126; Kellar, *Seth Bullock*, p. 116; *Black Hills Daily Times*, 11, 12, 13, 14 June 1891.

16. Driscoll, *Seventy Years of Banking*, pp. 77–78.

17. Helen Herrett, "Seth Bullock's Town," in *History of Butte County*, p. 22; Koller, "Minnesela-Belle Fourche Feud," p. 47; Driscoll, *Seventy Years of Banking*, p. 42; Varney, "History of the Chicago and North Western," pp. 59, 76–78; *Black Hills Daily Times*, 1 Dec. 1885; "Minnesela, DeMores, and the Start of Belle Fourche," p. 76.

18. Herrett, "Seth Bullock's Town," p. 22; "Belle Fourche, Bullock's Town," pp. 124–25.

19. Koller, "Minnesela Days," pp. 107–9; Koller, "Minnesela-Belle Fourche Feud," p. 47; "Minnesela, DeMores, and the Start of Belle Fourche," p. 76; "Belle Fourche, Bullock's Town," p. 128; Varney, "History of the Chicago and North Western," p. 78.

20. "Belle Fourche, Bullock's Town," p. 128; Koller, "Minnesela Days," pp. 108–9.

21. Stanley Bullock, "The Bullock Family," p. 12.

22. Ibid.; David Miller, "Black Hills Entrepreneur: Seth Bullock," in *South Dakota Leaders: From Pierre Chouteau, Jr., to Oscar Howe*, ed. Herbert T. Hoover & Larry J. Zimmerman (Vermillion: University of South Dakota Press, 1989), pp. 245–46; *Black Hills Daily Times*, 10 May 1881, 6 Feb., 28 Sept., 21 Dec. 1883, 2 Nov. 1884, 4 July, 2 Sept. 1885, 7 Aug. 1890, 1 July 1892, 1 Jan. 1895; *Deadwood Daily Pioneer-Times*, 10 Nov. 1898.

23. *Black Hills Daily Times*, 1 May, 22 June 1880, 13 Jan. 1883, 7 Sept., 12 Oct. 1884, 22 Oct. 1885, 29 July, 5 Aug. 1888, 26 Feb. 1890.

24. Ibid., 26 Sept., 2 Dec. 1886; Bob Lee, ed., *Gold, Gals, Guns, Guts: A History of Deadwood, Lead, and Spearfish, 1874–1976* (1976; reprint ed., Pierre: South Dakota State Historical Society Press, 2004), pp. 160–61.

25. Quoted in Travers D. Carman, "Captain Seth Bullock—A Black Hills Pioneer," *Outlook* 123 (29 Oct. 1919): 235.

26. *Black Hills Daily Times*, 11 Feb. 1891, 19 Apr. 1892.

27. George W. Kingsbury, *History of Dakota Territory*, and George Martin Smith, *South Dakota: Its History and Its People*, 5 vols. (Chicago: S. J. Clarke Publishing Co., 1915), 4:223; *Deadwood Daily Pioneer-Times*, 11 Oct. 1917; Butte County Property Records, Reference Book 4.

28. Kellar, *Seth Bullock*, pp. 11–12; Theodore Roosevelt, *An Autobiography* (New York: Macmillan Co., 1913), pp. 130–31. *See also* Roosevelt to John Hay, 9 Aug. 1903, in *The Letters of Theodore Roosevelt*, ed. Elting E. Morison, 8 vols. (Cambridge, Mass.: Harvard University Press, 1951–1954), 3:561, and Miller, "Black Hills Entrepreneur," p. 244.

29. Roosevelt to Hay, 9 Aug. 1903, p. 553; Roosevelt to Kermit Roosevelt, 18 Aug. 1906, in *Letters to Kermit from Theodore Roosevelt, 1902–1908*, ed. Will Irwin (New York: Charles Scribner's Sons, 1946), p. 150.

30. Roosevelt to Hay, 9 Aug. 1903, p. 553. *See also* Roosevelt, *Autobiography*, p. 130.

31. Roosevelt to Anna Roosevelt, 26 Aug. 1892, in *Letters of Theodore Roosevelt*, ed. Morison, 1:290.

32. Ibid.; *Black Hills Daily Times*, 26 Aug. 1892; Edmund Morris, *The Rise of Theodore Roosevelt* (New York: Modern Library, 2001), pp. 465–66.

33. *Black Hills Daily Times*, 6 Mar. 1894.

34. Ibid., 26 Sept. 1895.

35. "The Cowtown's Proudest Year," in *Pioneer Footprints*, p. 228.

CHAPTER 7: MOVING TO THE NATIONAL STAGE

1. *Deadwood Daily Pioneer-Times*, 4 Mar. 1905. *See also* Kenneth C. Kellar, *Seth Bullock: Frontier Marshal* (Aberdeen, S.Dak.: North Plains Press, 1972), p. 138.

2. *Deadwood Daily Pioneer-Times*, 11 Mar. 1905.

3. William A. Remer, Diary, 29 Oct. 1896, Adams Museum & House Archives, Deadwood, S.Dak.

4. *Black Hills Daily Times*, 3 Sept. 1896; *Deadwood Daily Pioneer-Times*, 14 Feb., 28 Mar. 1899.

5. *Black Hills Daily Times*, 9 Mar. 1881.

6. Ibid., 7 May 1891, 1 Apr., 12 Aug. 1892, 8 May 1896; *Deadwood Weekly Pioneer-Times*, 12 Dec. 1901; Watson Parker, *Deadwood: The Golden Years* (Lincoln: University of Nebraska Press, 1981), p. 76.

7. *Black Hills Daily Times*, 3 May 1895.

8. Ibid., 4 May 1895.

9. Ibid., 9 Jan., 24, 31 Mar., 8 May 1896; Remer Diary, 20 Jan. 1896; Dakota Hotel Company, "Articles of Incorporation," 5 Mar. 1896, Office of the Secretary of State, Domestic Articles of Incorporation Ledgers, 1878–1970, Box 24, 1896–1897, State Archives Collection, South Dakota State Historical Society, Pierre, S.Dak.

10. *Black Hills Daily Times*, 3, 24 Mar. 1896.

11. Ibid., 24 Apr., 8 May 1896.

12. Ibid., 31 Mar., 1 May 1896; *Deadwood Daily Pioneer-Times*, 21 Sept., 3 Oct. 1900, 16 June 1901; Mark S. Wolfe, *Boots on Bricks: A Walking Tour of Historic Downtown Deadwood* (Deadwood, S.Dak.: Deadwood Historic Preservation Commission, 1996), p. 66; "Dakota Hotel Company," Lawrence County Property Tax Records, 1899, Leland D. Case Library for Western Historical Studies, Black Hills State University, Spearfish, S.Dak.

13. *Black Hills Daily Times*, 24 Apr. 1897; *Deadwood Daily Pioneer-Times*, 20 Mar. 1898, 24 Feb. 1900; Remer Diary, 26 May 1898.

14. *Deadwood Daily Pioneer-Times*, 24 Feb. 1900.

15. Ibid., 18 Jan. 1901; Wolfe, *Boots on Bricks*, p. 67.

16. *Black Hills Daily Times*, 10 Nov. 1895; *Deadwood Daily Pioneer-Times*, 28 Sept., 11 Oct. 1906, 26 May 1914; *Deadwood Weekly Pioneer-Times*, 16 Dec. 1897; *Custer Weekly Chronicle*, 13 Oct. 1906.

17. *Black Hills Residence and Business Directory* (Deadwood, S.Dak.: Enterprise Printing Co., 1898), p. 25; *Black Hills Daily Times*, 14 Sept. 1893; *Deadwood Weekly Pioneer-Times*, 30 Sept., 7 Oct. 1897, 9 Jan. 1902; *Deadwood Daily Pioneer-Times*, 14 Oct., 12 Dec. 1899.

18. George P. Baldwin, ed., *The Black Hills Illustrated: A Terse Description of Conditions Past and Present of America's Greatest Mineral Belt* (Deadwood, S.Dak.: Black Hills Mining Men's Assoc., 1904), p. 129; *Black Hills Weekly Times*, 2, 16 Jan. 1897; *Black Hills Daily Times*, 24 Jan. 1897.

19. *Black Hills Weekly Times*, 16 Jan. 1897; *Black Hills Daily Times*, 13 Mar. 1897; *Deadwood Daily Pioneer-Times*, 3 June, 23 July 1897; *Deadwood Weekly Pioneer-Times*, 3 June, 19 Aug. 1897.

20. *Black Hills Daily Times*, 1 Apr., 6 Nov. 1896; *Deadwood Daily Pioneer-Times*, 3 June, 5 Aug. 1897; Remer Diary, 2 Nov. 1897.

21. Clifford P. Westermeier, *Who Rush to Glory: The Cowboy Volunteers of 1898* (Caldwell, Idaho: Caxton Printers, 1958), p. 40.

22. Ibid., pp. 29, 32–34, 39; Graham A. Cosmas, *An Army for*

Empire: The United States Army in the Spanish-American War (Columbia: University of Missouri Press, 1971), p. 133; Nathan Miller, *Theodore Roosevelt: A Life* (New York: William Morrow & Co., 1992), pp. 272–73.

23. *Denver Republican*, 25 Apr. 1898, quoted in Westermeier, *Who Rush to Glory*, p. 32.

24. Westermeier, *Who Rush to Glory*, p. 34; Miller, *Theodore Roosevelt*, p. 274; Edmund Morris, *The Rise of Theodore Roosevelt* (New York: Modern Library, 2001), pp. 642–43.

25. Otto L. Sues, *Grigsby's Cowboys: Third United States Volunteer Cavalry, Spanish-American War* (Salem, S.Dak.: James E. Patten, 1900), p. 12; Westermeier, *Who Rush to Glory*, pp. 70–71.

26. Sues, *Grigsby's Cowboys*, p. 127.

27. Ibid., pp. 10, 12, 14.

28. Quoted in Remer Diary, 29 Apr. 1898.

29. Sues, *Grigsby's Cowboys*, pp. 136, 148–51; Remer Diary, 7 May 1898.

30. *Chattanooga Times*, reprinted in *Deadwood Daily Pioneer-Times*, 2 Aug. 1898.

31. Sues, *Grigsby's Cowboys*, p. 140.

32. Remer Diary, 13 May 1898.

33. Sues, *Grigsby's Cowboys*, pp. 12, 16–17, 20–21; *Deadwood Daily Pioneer-Times*, 24 May 1895.

34. *Chicago Record*, reprinted in *Deadwood Daily Pioneer-Times*, 28 May 1898. *See also Deadwood Daily Pioneer-Times*, 24 May, 1 June 1898.

35. *Deadwood Daily Pioneer-Times*, 24 June 1898.

36. Ibid., 13 July 1898.

37. Ibid., 3 June 1898.

38. *Washington Post*, reprinted ibid., 26 June 1898.

39. *Deadwood Daily Pioneer-Times*, 18 June 1898. *See also* 15 June.

40. Ibid., 28 June 1898.

41. Ibid., 14 July 1898.

42. Ibid., 13 July 1898.

43. Quoted ibid., 31 July 1898.

44. Ibid., 24 June, 31 July 1898.

45. Ibid., 14, 24 Aug., 16, 17 Sept. 1898; Westermeier, *Who Rush to Glory*, pp. 210–11.

46. *Deadwood Daily Pioneer Times*, 17 Sept. 1898.

47. *Chicago Record-Herald*, reprinted in *Deadwood Weekly Pioneer-Times*, 4 Apr. 1901.

48. *Deadwood Daily Pioneer-Times*, 12 July 1899.

49. Ibid., 1 June 1899.

50. Ibid., 4, 15 Oct. 1899.

51. Ibid., 3, 4, 5 July 1901; *Deadwood Weekly Pioneer-Times*, 1 Aug. 1901.

52. Kermit Roosevelt, *The Happy Hunting-Grounds* (New York: Charles Scribner's Sons, 1920), pp. 175–76.

53. Theodore Roosevelt, *An Autobiography* (New York: Macmillan Co., 1913), p. 130.

54. Elting E. Morison, ed., *The Letters of Theodore Roosevelt*, 8 vols. (Cambridge, Mass.: Harvard University Press, 1951–1954), 2:1509; Morris, *Rise of Theodore Roosevelt*, pp. 770–71; *Iowa Reporter* (Waterloo), 21 Aug. 1900; *Deadwood Daily Pioneer-Times*, 15 Aug. 1900, 6 Mar. 1903.

55. Roosevelt, *Autobiography*, p. 142; Roosevelt, *Happy Hunting-Grounds*, pp. 157–58; Theodore Roosevelt to John Hay, 9 Aug. 1903, in *Letters of Theodore Roosevelt*, 3:558.

56. *Deadwood Daily Pioneer-Times*, 21 Sept. 1900.

57. Ibid., 4 Oct. 1900; *Anaconda Standard*, 4 Oct. 1900; *Deadwood Weekly Pioneer-Times*, 11 Oct. 1900.

58. Frank E. Nevins, quoted in *Deadwood Weekly Pioneer-Times*, 11 Oct. 1900.

59. *Deadwood Daily Pioneer-Times*, 10 Nov. 1900; Roosevelt to Charles Follen Mc Kim, 25 Apr. 1903, in *Letters of Theodore Roosevelt*, 3:470; Roosevelt to Hay, 9 Aug. 1903, 3:550–61; *Deadwood Weekly Pioneer-Times*, 30 Apr. 1903; *Custer Weekly Chronicle*, 21 Jan. 1905; Travers D. Carman, "Captain Seth Bullock—A Black Hills Pioneer," *Outlook* 123 (29 Oct. 1919): 234; Remer Diary, 1, 25 Apr. 1903; Edmund Morris, *Theodore Rex* (New York: Modern Library, 2002), p. 233.

60. *Custer Weekly Chronicle*, 1 Sept. 1906.

61. Theodore Roosevelt to Kermit Roosevelt, 1 Oct. 1907, in *Letters to Kermit from Theodore Roosevelt, 1902–1908*, ed. Will Irwin (New York: Charles Scribner's Sons, 1946), p. 216; *Custer Weekly Chronicle*, 26 Aug., 2 Sept. 1905, 25 Aug. 1906; Remer Diary, 21 Aug. 1903, 20 Aug. 1905; Carman, "Captain Seth Bullock," p. 235; *Deadwood Daily Pioneer-Times*, 22, 31 Aug. 1905; Kellar, *Seth Bullock*, pp.166–67; Roosevelt, *Happy Hunting-Grounds*, pp. 160–70. On page 160 of his book *Happy Hunting-Grounds*, Kermit Roosevelt says that he was fourteen when he first visited Bullock in the Black Hills, but he must not

have remembered correctly. Kermit was born in 1889, and his first visit was in 1905, making him sixteen.

CHAPTER 8: A FEDERAL MAN

1. Gifford Pinchot, *Breaking New Ground* (Seattle: University of Washington Press, 1947), pp. 116–17; Martha E. Geores, *Common Ground: The Struggle for Ownership of the Black Hills National Forest* (Lanham, Md.: Rowman & Littlefield Publishers, 1996), p. 40; Carl A. Newport, *A History of Black Hills Forestry: Forest Service Policies in Timber Management and Silviculture as They Affect the Lumber Industry* (Pierre: South Dakota Department of Game, Fish & Parks, 1956), pp. 16–18; Richmond L. Clow, "Timber Users, Timber Savers: Homestake Mining Company and the First Regulated Timber Harvest," *South Dakota History* 22 (Fall 1992): 222–23, 228–29; *Deadwood Weekly Pioneer*, 3 June 1897; *Black Hills Weekly Times*, 27 Feb., 6 Mar. 1897.

2. Pinchot, *Breaking New Ground*, pp. 130, 173–74, 255–56; Newport, *History of Black Hills Forestry*, pp. 18–20; Clow, "Timber Users, Timber Savers," pp. 226–31.

3. U.S., Department of Agriculture, Forest Service, *Black Hills National Forest: 50th Anniversary* (Washington, D.C.: Government Printing Office, 1948), p. 27; Clow, "Timber Users, Timber Savers," pp. 228–30; Geores, *Common Ground*, pp. 47–48; Newport, *History of Black Hills Forestry*, pp. 20, 24; *Deadwood Daily Pioneer-Times*, 18 Mar. 1898, 4 July, 21 Oct. 1899, 6 Mar., 12 June 1901.

4. *Deadwood Daily Pioneer-Times*, 12 June 1901.

5. Ibid., 1 May, 12 June 1901; Travers D. Carman, "Captain Seth Bullock—A Black Hills Pioneer," *Outlook* 123 (29 Oct. 1919): 234.

6. Theodore Roosevelt to Seth Bullock, 24 Sept. 1901, reproduced in Kenneth C. Kellar, *Seth Bullock: Frontier Marshal* (Aberdeen, S.Dak.: North Plains Press, 1972), pp. 121–22.

7. *Deadwood Daily Pioneer-Times*, 12 June 1901; Newport, *History of Black Hills Forestry*, pp. 19–20.

8. *Deadwood Weekly Pioneer-Times*, 14 Nov. 1901.

9. Quoted in Carman, "Captain Seth Bullock," p. 234. *See also* Kellar, *Seth Bullock*, p. 120.

10. *Deadwood Weekly Pioneer-Times*, 13 Feb. 1902.

11. Seth Bullock, "The Black Hills Forest Reserve," in *The Black Hills Illustrated: A Terse Description of Conditions Past and Present of America's Greatest Mineral Belt*, ed. George P. Baldwin (Deadwood, S.Dak.:

Black Hills Mining Men's Assoc., 1904), p. 63.

12. Ibid., pp. 63, 65; *Black Hills National Forest*, p. 22; Martha Linde, *Sawmills of the Black Hills* (Rapid City, S.Dak.: Jessie Y. Sundstrom, 1984), pp. 101–3.

13. *Deadwood Weekly Pioneer-Times*, 24 Apr. 1902.

14. Geores, *Common Ground*, pp. 48, 50–51; Newport, *History of Black Hills Forestry*, pp. 19, 21; *Deadwood Weekly Pioneer-Times*, 10 Apr. 1902; Linde, *Sawmills of the Black Hills*, p. 102; *Custer Weekly Chronicle*, 4 Nov. 1905.

15. Geores, *Common Ground*, pp. 44–46, 60–61; *Black Hills National Forest*, pp. 39–40; *Deadwood Daily Pioneer-Times*, 25 July 1905; *Custer Weekly Chronicle*, 13 May, 22 July 1905.

16. *Black Hills National Forest*, p. 20; Linde, *Sawmills of the Black Hills*, pp. 99–100; David Miller, "Black Hills Entrepreneur: Seth Bullock," in *South Dakota Leaders: From Pierre Chouteau, Jr., to Oscar Howe*, ed. Herbert T. Hoover & Larry J. Zimmerman (Vermillion: University of South Dakota Press, 1989), p. 243; Frank Thomson, *Ninety-Six Years in the Black Hills* (Detroit, Mich.: Harlo Press, 1974), pp. 72, 185; *Custer Weekly Chronicle*, 30 Sept. 1905.

17. Linde, *Sawmills of the Black Hills*, pp. 99–100; *Custer Weekly Chronicle*, 26 Aug., 16 Sept. 1905.

18. *Deadwood Daily Pioneer-Times*, 12 Oct. 1905.

19. *Custer Weekly Chronicle*, 4 Feb., 27 May 1905; Miller, "Black Hills Entrepreneur," p. 244.

20. Quoted in *Custer Weekly Chronicle*, 30 Sept. 1905.

21. *Deadwood Daily Pioneer-Times*, 1 May 1901, 12 Aug. 1905; *Deadwood Weekly Pioneer-Times*, 16 May 1901; *Custer Weekly Chronicle*, 26 Aug. 1905, 27 Jan. 1906; Miller, "Black Hills Entrepreneur," pp. 243–44; John W. Bohi, "Seventy-Five Years at Wind Cave: A History of the National Park," *South Dakota Historical Collections* 31 (1962): 420, 422, 424, 431.

22. Miller, "Black Hills Entrepreneur," pp. 243–44; Gail Evans-Hatch and Michael Evans-Hatch, *Place of Passages: Jewel Cave National Monument Historic Resource Study* (Omaha, Nebr.: Midwestern Region National Park Service, 2006), pp. 173–74.

23. Theodore Roosevelt, *An Autobiography* (New York: Macmillan Co., 1913), p. 431.

24. Ibid., pp. 432, 434; Robert G. Dunbar, *Forging New Rights in Western Waters* (Lincoln: University of Nebraska Press, 1983), pp.

50–52; Raymond Y. Chapman, "History of the Belle Fourche Irrigation Project" (M.A. thesis, University of South Dakota, 1931), pp. 5,
12. Some sources, i.e., Joe Koller, "History of Orman Dam in Butte
County South Dakota," in *Cowboys and Sodbusters* ([Vale, S.Dak.]:
n.p., [1963]), p. 251, state that the Belle Fourche project was the first
or second federal reclamation project authorized, but they do not
appear to be correct.

25. Roosevelt, *Autobiography*, p. 434.

26. "Peter P. Vallery," in *Pioneer Footprints*, 3d ed. (Belle Fourche,
S.Dak.: Black Hills Half Century Club, 1964), p. 46; Chapman,
"History of the Belle Fourche Irrigation Project," pp. 9–11; Marvin
P. Riley, W. F. Kumlien, and Duane Tucker, *50 Years Experience on the
Belle Fourche Irrigation Project*, South Dakota Agricultural Experiment
Station, Bulletin no. 450 (Brookings: South Dakota State College,
1955), p. 12n10; Belle Fourche Valley Water Users Association to E. A.
Hitchcock, 27 June 1906, Newell Museum, Newell, S.Dak.; "U and I
Sugar Company," in *A History of Butte County, South Dakota*, comp. Pat
Engebretson, Kay Heck, & Helen Herrett (Dallas, Tex.: Curtis Media
Corp., 1989), pp. 95–96.

27. *Deadwood Daily Pioneer-Times*, 12 Aug. 1905.

28. *Custer Weekly Chronicle*, 21 Jan. 1905.

29. Ibid., 14, 21 Jan. 1905.

30. *Deadwood Daily Pioneer-Times*, 15 Jan. 1905.

31. Ibid., 5 Dec. 1905.

32. Ibid., 5, 7, 8, 26 Dec. 1905; *Custer Weekly Chronicle*, 9 Dec. 1905.

33. Quoted in *Deadwood Daily Pioneer-Times*, 28 Dec. 1905.

34. *Queen City Mail*, reprinted ibid., 16 Dec. 1905.

35. *Deadwood Daily Pioneer-Times*, 7 Dec. 1905.

36. Ibid., 15 Aug., 24 Oct., 16 Dec. 1905; *Custer Weekly Chronicle*, 3
Mar. 1906; Linde, *Sawmills of the Black Hills*, pp. 101–2; Geores, *Common Ground*, p. 60; Kellar, *Seth Bullock*, p. 130.

37. *Deadwood Daily Pioneer-Times*, 7 Dec. 1905.

38. Ibid., 23 Dec. 1905; *Custer Weekly Chronicle*, 10 Feb. 1906; Kellar, *Seth Bullock*, p. 124; Seth Bullock to the Attorney General, 12 Jan.
1907, Box 99, Location 230/31/35/07, Letters Received, Records of
the Department of Justice, Record Group 60, National Archives and
Records Administration, Washington, D.C.

39. Frederick S. Calhoun, *The Lawmen: United States Marshals and
Their Deputies, 1789–1989* (Washington, D.C.: Smithsonian Institu-

tion Press, 1989), p. 3; Kermit Roosevelt, *The Happy Hunting-Grounds* (New York: Charles Scribner's Sons, 1920), p. 155.

40. Bullock to Kermit Roosevelt, 19 Apr. 1909, Kermit Roosevelt and Belle Roosevelt Papers, 1885–1975 (hereafter cited as Roosevelt Papers), Manuscript Division, Library of Congress, Washington, D.C.

41. Bullock to Attorney General, 12 Jan. 1907.

42. Carman, "Captain Seth Bullock," p. 233.

43. Quoted in Roosevelt, *Happy Hunting-Grounds*, p. 176.

44. Roosevelt, *Autobiography*, pp. 52, 54; Lawrence F. Abbott, ed., *The Letters of Archie Butt, Personal Aide to President Roosevelt* (New York: Doubleday, Page & Co., 1924), pp. 368–69.

45. Roosevelt, *Autobiography*, p. 131.

46. Quoted in Estelline Bennett, *Old Deadwood Days* (1928; reprint ed., Lincoln: University of Nebraska Press, 1982), p. 54.

47. Quoted in Carman, "Captain Seth Bullock," pp. 234–35. This material is repeated in Kellar, *Seth Bullock*, pp. 163–65.

48. Kellar, *Seth Bullock*, pp. 168–73.

49. Bullock to Kermit Roosevelt, 29 Oct. 1916, Roosevelt Papers.

50. Bullock to Kermit Roosevelt, 10 July 1917, ibid.; Jean McLeod Doughty, "The Suffrage Movement in Lawrence County," in *Some History of Lawrence County* (Deadwood, S.Dak.: Lawrence County Historical Society, 1981), pp. 655–56.

51. Bullock to Kermit Roosevelt, 29 Oct. 1916.

52. Roosevelt, *Happy Hunting-Grounds*, p. 177; Bullock to Kermit Roosevelt, 10 July 1917; Miller, "Black Hills Entrepreneur," p. 246; Nathan Miller, *Theodore Roosevelt: A Life* (New York: William Morrow & Co., 1992), p. 539; Kellar, *Seth Bullock*, p. 178.

53. *Deadwood Daily Pioneer-Times*, 25 May 1917; Kellar, *Seth Bullock*, pp. 178–79.

54. Bullock to Kermit Roosevelt, 10 July 1917.

55. Ibid., 4 Aug. 1918, Roosevelt Papers.

56. Roosevelt, *Happy Hunting-Grounds*, p. 180.

57. Carman, "Captain Seth Bullock," p. 235.

58. Quoted in *Deadwood Daily Pioneer-Times*, 6 July 1919.

59. Ibid., 4, 6 July 1919; Roosevelt, *Happy Hunting-Grounds*, pp. 180–81; Kellar, *Seth Bullock*, p. 183.

60. *Deadwood Daily Pioneer-Times*, 24, 27 Sept. 1919.

Bibliography

BOOKS

Abbott, Lawrence F., ed. *The Letters of Archie Butt, Personal Aide to President Roosevelt.* New York: Doubleday, Page & Co., 1924.

Andrea's Historical Atlas of Dakota. Chicago: A. T. Andreas, 1884.

Baldwin, George P., ed. *The Black Hills Illustrated: A Terse Description of Conditions Past and Present of America's Greatest Mineral Belt.* Deadwood, S.Dak.: Black Hills Mining Men's Assoc., 1904.

Bennett, Estelline. *Old Deadwood Days.* 1928. Reprint ed. Lincoln: University of Nebraska Press, 1982.

The Black Hills of Dakota, 1881. Deadwood, S.Dak.: Deadwood Board of Trade, 1881.

Black Hills Residence and Business Directory. Deadwood, S.Dak.: Enterprise Printing Co., 1898.

Brown, Jesse, and A. M. Willard. *The Black Hills Trails: A History of the Struggles of the Pioneers in the Winning of the Black Hills.* Ed. John T. Milek. Rapid City, S.Dak.: Rapid City Journal Co., 1924.

[Bullock, Seth]. *Seth Bullock's The Founding of a County: A Historical Sketch of Lawrence County, South Dakota, from His Records of 1876.* Comp. P. H. Kellar. Deadwood, S.Dak.: By the Compiler, 1986.

Calhoun, Frederick S. *The Lawmen: United States Marshals and Their Deputies, 1789–1989.* Washington, D.C.: Smithsonian Institution Press, 1989.

Casey, Robert J. *The Black Hills and Their Incredible Characters.* Indianapolis: Bobbs Merrill Co., 1949.

Clem, Alan L., and James M. Rumbolz. *Law Enforcement: The South Dakota Experience.* Sturgis: South Dakota Peace Officers' Assoc., 1982.

Clow, Richmond L. *Chasing the Glitter: Black Hills Milling, 1874–1959.* Historical Preservation Series, no. 2. Pierre: South Dakota State Historical Society Press, 2002.

Cosmas, Graham A. *An Army for Empire: The United States Army in the Spanish–American War.* Columbia: University of Missouri Press, 1971.

Cramton, Louis C. *Early History of Yellowstone National Park and Its Relation to National Park Policies.* United States Department of the

Interior. Washington, D.C.: Government Printing Office, 1932.

Driscoll, R. E. *Seventy Years of Banking in the Black Hills*. Rapid City, S.Dak.: Gate City Guide, 1948.

Dunbar, Robert G. *Forging New Rights in Western Waters*. Lincoln: University of Nebraska Press, 1983.

Engebretson, Pat, Kay Heck, and Helen Herrett, comps. *A History of Butte County, South Dakota*. Dallas, Tex.: Curtis Media Corp., 1989.

Evans-Hatch, Gail, and Michael Evans-Hatch. *Place of Passages: Jewel Cave National Monument Historic Resource Study*. Omaha, Nebr.: Midwestern Region National Park Service, 2006.

Fielder, Mildred. *Railroads of the Black Hills*. New York: Bonanza Books, 1964.

————. *Silver is the Fortune*. Aberdeen, S.Dak.: North Plains Press, 1978.

Geores, Martha E. *Common Ground: The Struggle for Ownership of the Black Hills National Forest*. Lanham, Md.: Rowman & Littlefield Publishers, 1996.

Hafnor, John. *Black Hills Believables: Items Panned from the Golden Past of Paha Sapa*. Billings, Mont.: Falcon Press Publishing Co., 1983.

Haines, Aubrey L. *The Yellowstone Story: A History of Our First National Park*. 2 vols. Yellowstone National Park, Wyo.: Yellowstone Library & Museum Assoc., 1977.

Irving, J. D. *Economic Resources of the Northern Black Hills*. United States Geological Survey, Professional Paper no. 26. Washington: Government Printing Office, 1904.

Kellar, Kenneth C. *Seth Bullock: Frontier Marshal*. Aberdeen, S.Dak.: North Plains Press, 1972.

Kingsbury, George W. *History of Dakota Territory*, and George Martin Smith, *South Dakota: Its History and Its People*. 5 vols. Chicago: S. J. Clarke Publishing Co., 1915.

Klock, Irma H. *All Roads Lead to Deadwood*. Lead, S.Dak.: By the Author, 1979.

Lamar, Howard Robert. *Dakota Territory, 1861–1889: A Study of Frontier Politics*. New Haven, Conn.: Yale University Press, 1956.

Lee, Bob, ed. *Gold, Gals, Guns, Guts: A History of Deadwood, Lead, and Spearfish, 1874–1976*. 1976. Reprint ed. Pierre: South Dakota State Historical Society Press, 2004.

————, and Dick Williams. *Last Grass Frontier: The South Dakota*

Stock Grower Heritage. Sturgis, S.Dak.: Black Hills Publishers, 1964.

Lee, Robert. Fort Meade & the Black Hills. Lincoln: University of Nebraska Press, 1991.

Leeson, M. A. History of Montana, 1739–1885. Chicago: Warner, Beers & Co., 1885.

Linde, Martha. Sawmills of the Black Hills. Rapid City, S.Dak.: Jessie Y. Sundstrom, 1984.

Lubetkin, M. John. Jay Cooke's Gamble: The Northern Pacific Railroad, the Sioux, and the Panic of 1873. Norman: University of Oklahoma Press, 2006.

Malone, Michael P., and Richard B. Roeder. Montana: A History of Two Centuries. Seattle: University of Washington Press, 1976.

McClintock, John S. Pioneer Days in the Black Hills: Accurate History and Facts Related by One of the Early Day Pioneers. Ed. Edward L. Senn. 1939. Reprint ed. Norman: University of Oklahoma Press, 2000.

McLaird, James D. Wild Bill Hickok and Calamity Jane: Deadwood Legends. South Dakota Biography Series, no. 2. Pierre: South Dakota State Historical Society Press, 2008.

Miller, Nathan. Theodore Roosevelt: A Life. New York: William Morrow & Co., 1992.

Morris, Edmund. The Rise of Theodore Roosevelt. New York: Modern Library, 2001.

————. Theodore Rex. New York: Modern Library, 2002.

Newport, Carl A. A History of Black Hills Forestry: Forest Service Policies in Timber Management and Silviculture as They Affect the Lumber Industry. Pierre: South Dakota Department of Game, Fish & Parks, 1956.

Parker, Watson. Deadwood: The Golden Years. Lincoln: University of Nebraska Press, 1981.

Paul, Rodman Wilson. Mining Frontiers of the Far West, 1848–1880. New York: Holt, Rinehart & Winston, 1963.

Pinchot, Gifford. Breaking New Ground. Seattle: University of Washington Press, 1947.

Pioneer Footprints. 3d ed. Belle Fourche, S.Dak.: Black Hills Half Century Club, 1973.

Quiett, Glenn Chesney. Pay Dirt: A Panorama of American Gold-Rushes. New York: D. Appleton-Century Co., 1936.

Riley, Marvin P., W. F. Kumlien, and Duane Tucker. 50 Years Experience on the Belle Fourche Irrigation Project. South Dakota Agricultural Experiment Station, Bulletin no. 450. Brookings:

South Dakota State College, 1955.

Roosevelt, Kermit. *The Happy Hunting-Grounds.* New York: Charles Scribner's Sons, 1920.

Roosevelt, Theodore. *An Autobiography.* New York: Macmillan Co., 1913.

_____. *The Letters of Theodore Roosevelt.* Ed. Elting E. Morison. 8 vols. Cambridge, Mass.: Harvard University Press, 1951–1954.

_____. *Letters to Kermit from Theodore Roosevelt, 1902–1908.* Ed. Will Irwin. New York: Charles Scribner's Sons, 1946.

Schell, Herbert. *History of South Dakota.* 4th ed., rev. John E. Miller. Pierre: South Dakota State Historical Society Press, 2004.

Schullery, Paul. *Searching for Yellowstone: Ecology and Wonder in the Last Wilderness.* Boston: Houghton Mifflin Co., 1997.

Some History of Lawrence County. Deadwood, S.Dak.: Lawrence County Historical Society, 1981.

Spence, Clark C. *Territorial Politics and Government in Montana, 1864–89.* Urbana: University of Illinois Press, 1975.

Sues, Otto L. *Grigsby's Cowboys: Third United States Volunteer Cavalry, Spanish-American War.* Salem, S.Dak.: James E. Patten, 1900.

Tallent, Annie D. *The Black Hills; or, The Last Hunting Ground of the Dakotahs.* 2d ed. Sioux Falls, S.Dak.: Brevet Press, 1974.

Thomson, Frank. *Ninety-Six Years in the Black Hills.* Detroit, Mich.: Harlo Press, 1974.

U.S. Department of Agriculture. Forest Service. *Black Hills National Forest: 50th Anniversary.* Washington, D.C.: Government Printing Office, 1948.

Warren, Louis S. *Buffalo Bill's America: William Cody and the Wild West Show.* New York: Alfred A. Knopf, 2005.

Waterland, Joel K. *The Mines Around & Beyond: The History of the Deadwood, Two Bit, . . . and Tinton Mining Districts, Black Hills of South Dakota.* Lead, S.Dak.: By the Author, 1991.

_____. *The Spawn & the Mother Lode: The Story of the Placer, Conglomerate and Precambrian Mines of the Central City, Lead and Deadwood Area.* Lead, S.Dak.: By the Author, 1987.

Westermeier, Clifford P. *Who Rush to Glory: The Cowboy Volunteers of 1898.* Caldwell, Idaho: Caxton Printers, 1958.

Wolfe, Mark S. *Boots on Bricks: A Walking Tour of Historic Downtown Deadwood.* Deadwood, S.Dak.: Deadwood Historic Preservation Commission, 1996.

Young, Harry ("Sam"). *Hard Knocks: A Life Story of the Vanishing West.* 1915. Reprint ed. Pierre: South Dakota State Historical Society Press, 2005.

ARTICLES

Anderson, Harry H. "Deadwood, South Dakota: An Effort at Stability." *Montana, the Magazine of Western History* 20 (Jan. 1970): 40–47.

Ball, Larry D. "A Contractor's Cussedness: Politics, Labor, Law, and the Keets Mine Incident of 1877." *South Dakota History* 26 (Summer/Fall 1996): 93–120.

Bohi, John W. "Seventy-Five Years at Wind Cave: A History of the National Park." *South Dakota Historical Collections* 31 (1962): 365–468.

Bullock, Seth. "An Account of Deadwood and the Northern Black Hills in 1876." Ed. Harry H. Anderson. *South Dakota Historical Collections* 31 (1962): 287–364.

_____. "The Black Hills Forest Reserve." In *The Black Hills Illustrated: A Terse Description of Conditions Past and Present of America's Greatest Mineral Belt.* Ed. George P. Baldwin. Deadwood, S.Dak.: Black Hills Mining Men's Assoc., 1904. Pp. 63–65.

_____. "Early Day Bandits." *Black Hills Daily Pioneer-Times,* 3–9 May 1902.

Carman, Travers D. "Captain Seth Bullock—A Black Hills Pioneer." *Outlook* 123 (29 Oct. 1919): 233–36.

Clow, Richmond L. "Timber Users, Timber Savers: Homestake Mining Company and the First Regulated Timber Harvest." *South Dakota History* 22 (Fall 1992): 213–37.

Floyd, Laura. "Deadwood's Political Star." *Deadwood Magazine* (Nov. 2006): 13–17.

Koller, Joe. "History of Orman Dam in Butte County, South Dakota." In *Cowboys and Sodbusters.* [Vale, S.Dak.]: n.p., [1963]. Pp. 251–55.

_____. "Minnesela Days." *South Dakota Historical Collections* 24 (1949): 1–113.

Mason, Kathy S. "Adapting to Endure: The Early Years of Wind Cave National Park, 1903–1916." *South Dakota History* 32 (Summer 2002): 149–64.

Miller, David. "Black Hills Entrepreneur: Seth Bullock." In *South*

Dakota Leaders: From Pierre Chouteau, Jr., to Oscar Howe. Ed. Herbert
T. Hoover & Larry J. Zimmerman. Vermillion: University of
South Dakota Press, 1989. Pp. 232–48.

Pettigrew, R[ichard] F. "Pettigrew Visits the Black Hills." *The
Sunshine State* 7 (Mar. 1926): 38–41.

Rice, W. G. "Deadwood's Influence on the Development of the
Black Hills." *Black Hills Engineer* 18 (Jan. 1930): 53–60.

Richardson, Leander P. "A Trip to the Black Hills." *Scribner's Monthly*
13 (Apr. 1877): 748–56.

Wolff, David A. "Black Hills in Transition." In *A New South Dakota
History.* Ed. Harry F. Thompson. Sioux Falls, S.Dak.: Center for
Western Studies, 2005. Pp. 288–317.

————. "No Matter How You Do It, Fraud is Fraud: Another
Look at Black Hills Mining Scandals." *South Dakota History* 33
(Summer 2003): 91–119.

————. "Pyritic Smelting at Deadwood: A Temporary Solution to
Refractory Ores." *South Dakota History* 15 (Winter 1985): 312–39.

NEWSPAPERS

Anaconda Standard, 1900.

Black Hills Daily Times, 1877–1897.

Black Hills Pioneer, 1876–1877.

Black Hills Weekly and Whitewood Plaindealer, 1939.

Black Hills Weekly Times, 1877–1897.

Butte Miner, 1876.

Custer Weekly Chronicle, 1905–1906.

Deadwood Daily Pioneer-Times, 1897–1919.

Deadwood Weekly Pioneer-Times, 1897–1919.

Deadwood Pioneer-Times, 1952.

Helena Daily Herald, 1867–1873.

Helena Daily Independent, 1874–1876.

Helena Weekly Herald, 1875.

Iowa Reporter (Waterloo), 1900.

Sturgis Weekly Record, 1886.

UNPUBLISHED SOURCES

Adams Museum & House Archives, Deadwood, S.Dak.
  George E. Hair to Bob Crow, 24 Nov. 1926, Box 139.
  Seth Bullock File.

William A. Remer, Diary, 1896–1943.

American Heritage Center, University of Wyoming, Laramie, Wyo.
    Seth Bullock to Edward Seymour, 13 Aug. 1918, Edmund
    Seymour Collection.

Butte County Courthouse, Belle Fourche, S.Dak.
    Butte County Property Records.

Canada. Census of Canada East, Canada West, New Brunswick, and
    Nova Scotia, 1851. *AncestryLibrary.com*.

Lawrence County Courthouse, Deadwood, S.Dak.
    Lawrence County Property Records, 1881–1905.
    Leland D. Case Library for Western Historical Studies,
    Black Hills State University, Spearfish, S.Dak.
    Lawrence County Property Tax Records, 1881–1905.

Library of Congress, Manuscript Division, Washington, D.C.
    Kermit Roosevelt and Belle Roosevelt Papers, 1885–1975.

Maureen and Mike Mansfield Library, University of Montana,
    Missoula, Mont., http://nwda-db.wsulibs.wsu.edu.
    Teresa Hamann, "Guide to the Execution Invitations
    Collection, 1875–1922."

Newell Museum, Newell, S.Dak.
    Belle Fourche Valley Water Users Association to E. A.
    Hitchcock, 27 June 1906.

North Dakota State Archives and Library, Bismarck, N.Dak.
    John Pennington Papers.

South Dakota State Historical Society, State Archives Collection,
    Pierre, S.Dak.
    Alfalfa Controversy File.
    Office of the Secretary of State, Domestic Articles of
    Incorporation Ledgers, 1878–1970.

U.S. Bureau of Land Management
    Government Land Patent Records. www.glorecords.blm.
    gov.

U.S. Department of Interior. Census Office.
    Manuscript census, Lawrence County, Pennington County,
    Dak. 1880.

U. S. National Archives and Records Administration, Washington, D.C.
    Letters Received, Records of the Justice Department,
    Record Group 60.

THESES

Chapman, Raymond Y. "History of the Belle Fourche Irrigation Project." M.A. thesis, University of South Dakota, 1931.

Varney, Michael Edgar. "The History of the Chicago and North Western Railway's Black Hills Division." M.A. thesis, University of Wyoming, 1963.

Index

Numbers in **bold** indicate photographs.